African American Women Administrators

Annette W. Rusher

University Press of America, Inc.
Lanham • New York • London

Copyright © 1996 by
University Press of America,® Inc.
4720 Boston Way
Lanham, Maryland 20706

3 Henrietta Street
London, WC2E 8LU England

All rights reserved
Printed in the United States of America
British Cataloging in Publication Information Available

Library of Congress Cataloging-in-Publication Data

Rusher, Annette W.
African American women administrators / Annette W. Rusher.
p. cm.
Includes bibliographical references.
1. Women college administrators--United States. 2. Afro-American college administrators.
LB2341.R75   1996   371.1'11'082--dc20   95-26708 CIP

ISBN 0-7618-0249-5 (cloth: alk. ppr.)
ISBN 0-7618-0250-9 (pbk: alk. ppr.)

∞™ The paper used in this publication meets the minimum
requirements of American National Standard for information
Sciences—Permanence of Paper for Printed Library Materials,
ANSI Z39.48—1984

Contents

Preface		vii
Acknowledgments		ix
I.	NATURE AND PURPOSE OF STUDY	1
	A. Introduction	1
	B. Background	2
	1. The Invisible National Problem	2
	2. Consequences Associated with Being An African American Woman Administrator	3
	3. African American Women Educators	3
	C. Statement of the Problem	4
	D. Theoretical Framework	5
	1. Human Capital Theory	5
	E. Purpose of the Study	6
	F. Significance	7
	G. Assumptions and Initial Expectations	8
	H. Guiding Questions	9
	I. Methodology	9
	1. Research Subjects	9
	2. Research Design	10
	3. Primary Research Methods	10
	4. Pretest	11
	5. Study Implementation	12
	J. Limitations	12
	K. Data Analysis	13
	L. Summary	14

II.	REVIEW OF LITERATURE		15
	A.	Introduction	15
	B.	A Brief History of African American Women Administrators in Higher Education	15
		1. African American Administrator Shortages	18
		2. Increased Employment Opportunities	19
		3. Declined Interest in Higher Education	20
		4. Decreased Financial Aid	20
	C.	Recruitment of African American Women Administrators	21
	D.	Retention of African American Women Administrators	22
	E.	Promotion of African American Women Administrators in Higher Education	23
	G.	The Theory of Human Capital	24
		1. Introduction	24
		2. Definition of Human Capital	24
		3. History of Human Capital	25
		4. Explanation of Accumulated Human Capital	26
		5. Research on Human Capital	28
		6. Usages of Human Capital Theory	29
		7. Schools of Human Capital Theory	30
	H.	Summary	33
III.	METHODOLOGY		35
	A.	Research Approach and Rationale	35
		1. Quantitative Method	35
		2. Qualitative Method	36
		3. Definition of Terms	36
		4. Selecting A Topic	37
		5. Population, Sample, and Sampling Procedures	38
	B.	Research Questions	38
	C.	Data Collection Procedures	39
		1. Difficulties Obtaining Information	39
	D.	Survey Format	41
		1. Design of Survey Instrument	41
		2. Survey Pretest	42

		3.	Instrumentation	42
		4.	Cost of Survey	43
		5.	Management and Synthesis of Data	43
	E.	Data Analysis and Interpretation		44
		1.	Statistical Analysis	44
	F.	Problems of Reliability and Validity		45
		1.	Reliability and Validity	45
	G.	Summary		46
IV.	PRESENTATION AND DISCUSSION OF SUBJECTS			47
	A.	Profile of Subjects		48
		1.	Current Position	48
		2.	Institutions	48
		3.	Table 1 - Background of Respondents	50
		4.	Basic Demographics	49
		5.	Previous Experience and Promotion History	49
		6.	Previous Education	51
	B.	Administrators Tasks and Functions		52
		1.	Scholarly and Creative Activities	52
		2.	Professional Involvement	53
		3.	Professional Service	52
	C.	Administrative Attitudes		53
	D.	TWI/HBI Characteristics		57
		1.	Promotions	57
		2.	Previous Education	57
	E.	Summary		58
V.	STATISTICAL DATA ANALYSIS			59
	A.	Elaboration		59
	B.	Research Questions Analyzed		60
	C.	Internal and External Factors used in Analysis		60
	D.	Results for Guiding Question 1		61
		Summary of Data Analysis for Guiding Question 1		62
	E.	Results for Guiding Question 2		62
		Summary of Data Analysis for Guiding Question 2		67
	F.	Results for Guiding Question 3		68
		Summary of Data Analysis for Guiding Question 3		74

VI. DISCUSSION AND RECOMMENDATIONS		77
A.	Overview	77
B.	Discussion of Subjects	78
C.	Discussion of Statistical Data Analysis	80
D.	Internal and External Factors Introduced as Control Variables	83
E.	Concluding Comments	85
F.	Recommendations	86
APPENDICES		89
A.	Informational Letter to Organizations	89
B.	Survey Letter	90
C.	Complimentary Print Card	91
D.	Survey Reminder Cards	92
E.	Respondent's Comments	92
REFERENCES		101
VITA		109

Preface

The number of African American women administrators in higher education is not impressive. Although several institutions have implemented aggressive recruitment programs to attract and retain minorities, their efforts have not resulted in significant increases in the number of African American women administrators.

Although the actual account of African American Women Administrators is low, however, the number of qualified African American women in higher education is more than sufficient. African American women are in the pipeline but are not present throughout the ranks of higher education administration. Thus, the question must be raised about the recruitment, retention, and promotion patterns of African American women in higher education.

This exploratory study examines the recruitment, retention, and promotion patterns of 154 African American women administrators in the position of dean and above (with and without tenure). The women participating in the study were over 40 years of age, married with children, and felt good about working at their institutions. They do not engage in networking or belong to support groups, but do have mentors.

Acknowledgments

The author gratefully acknowledges the presene of a her Heavenly Father, the assistance of her dissertation committee, Dr. Ella Simmons, Dr. Eleanor Love, Dr. Denise Gifford, Dr. Gloria Murray, and Dr. Joseph Petrosko for their continued guidance, support and encouragement. Special thanks to Dr. Ella Simmons, a "student's professor", mentor and friend, Dr. Gordon Ruscoe, who served as a "beacon of light" in a sea of darkness. Special appreciation is extended to the African American women administrators who eagerly gave of their time to participate in this study. Al Liang for his outstanding analytical support. I acknowledge my mother, Annie Mae Williams (deceased) for her strong belief in educating her seven children, my sisters, Beverly Williams Prince and Wendolyn Sue Maxwell for their roles as surrogate parents, my husband, Cpt. Robert E. Rusher (deceased), other family members and friends.

Chapter I

Nature and Purpose of the Study

Introduction

History reveals that the black female has pioneered and forged new frontiers in education as leaders and as participants. This was most evident in the 1800s after the right to learn to read and write was permissible for slaves and ex-slaves. Many of the early primary schools and colleges were established by and for black females. However, given the approximate 100-150-year existence of the 117 historically black colleges and universities in existence today, less than 10 percent have African American female chief academic officers or presidents. Therein lies the dilemma facing African American in higher education (Gill & Showell, 1991, p. 2)

The above observations are still relevant today. There is a paucity of black females in higher education, specifically in positions of academic leadership and responsibility. The opportunity to study such women administrators, in numbers and content similar to men is still not available (Harvard, 1986). Professional organizations in higher education do not maintain statistical data on women of ethnic groups.

A well established myth in American higher education administration is that black women simply do not exist. Williams (1986) found that there is a small but growing body of literature about black women in administration at predominantly white colleges. The increasing number of black women college administrators at these two institutions is a new phenomenon. Before the 1970s there was nothing to write concerning the existence of African American women in administration due to the fact that there were none; college administrators were white males.

Myrtis Mosley (1980) did one of the first studies of black women college administrators at predominantly white institutions. Mosley discovered in her study that the majority of women were in staff positions, without mentors, and were doubtful about their career progression. Davis (1980; 1981) and Giddings (1985) revealed through their study the need for further research on the accomplishments and present status of black women in a variety of fields.

This study is an exploratory and descriptive examination of African American women administrators at various historically black institutions (HBIs) and traditionally white institutions (TWIs). The primary purpose and focus of this study is to acquire a better understanding of the recruitment, retention, and promotion patterns from the perspective of African American women administrators in the position of dean and or higher ranking position (with or without tenure).

Background

Title VII of the 1964 U.S. Civil Rights Act outlawed employment discrimination based on race, gender, and other defined attributes (Fosu, 1992). In 1965 "affirmative action" was established by Executive Order 11246 to oversee the hiring and promotion practices of federal contracts with specific regard to blacks. Employers were mandated to adopt written formal goals and a specific timetable for accomplishment of these goals, and the Executive Order was eventually extended to women as a group in 1972. In view of the legislative procedures that have been put in place to ensure that women and minorities are considered for all employment opportunities, the black female is still not visible in administration at most institutions of higher education.

The Invisible National Problem

The presence of African American women in higher education has been called the "invisible problem." The shortage of these women is not new. It is but a portion of a longstanding problem- -African American educator shortages in general (Darling-Hammond, 1987). According to the American Council on Education/Office of Minority Concern (ACE/OMC [1987]), there has never been an adequate supply of African

American educators of either gender, especially in the rural south (Anderson, 1988).

African American women, like their white sisters, are often "tokens" in the system of higher education. In such positions African American women may constantly fight stereotypes that force them into playing limited and caricatured roles (Kanter 1977, 1992; Carroll, 1982; & Powell, 1987). Dumas (1980) concludes that even when black women exhibit a certain level of occupational sophistication and leadership potential, they often play symbolic roles while being denied the exercise of significant power. African American women often have difficulty balancing expectations and demands attached to their symbolic roles and those that come with their professional status and responsibilities. Epstein (1973, 1987) suggests that the black woman administrator should have a place in the organizational structure and be guaranteed a secure position in the normal exchange system of that pattern of power.

Consequences Associated With Being an African American Woman Administrator

The experiences described here and elsewhere reveal a genuine insensitivity to African American women's needs for support and reassurance, which can challenge their own identity and threaten their inner security. Many African Americans in higher education have commented that a person is only a black women administrator in a white institution (Williams, 1982). African American women at HBIs are not identified primarily by their ethnic group but by their position title and accomplishments.

If they are to achieve full partnership, African American women must be astute and learn all they can about the institution's culture and become active participants in this environment. The ultimate challenge for the black woman administrator is to be the administrator who happens to be a black woman. If this kind of thinking takes precedence, black women will not be "tokens," but will be viewed as part of the institutional landscape.

Advances for African American Women Educators

In spite of how the black woman administrator was depicted by earlier researchers, recent statistics reveal an increase in women and minorities in higher education positions of leadership. The turbulence and unrest of the 1960s brought about many changes in higher education. In the 1960s, the Johnson Administration was directly responsible for the upsurge of participation of minorities in higher education. Many minority administrators were appointed as directors of programs specifically established for minority and disadvantaged students, i.e., Upward Bound, Trio, and Affirmative Action (Wilson, 1987). In the 1970s, black (male and female) administrators comprised 7.4 percent of positions in higher education.

However, the fundamental truth is that, while minorities continue to grow both in numbers and as a proportion of the U.S. population, they remain underrepresented in higher education. Thus, there is a relative absence of black female leadership at both predominantly white and predominantly black institutions. Current data suggest that black females are earning degrees at increasing rates. At the bachelor's degree level, black women comprise 62 percent, while black men comprise 38 percent. Master's degrees earned by black women comprise 64 percent compared to 36 percent for black men. As at these levels, for example, the number of black females has begun to surpasses the number of black males on the doctoral level. These statistics indicate that the numbers of qualified black females do not coincide with the numbers of black females in leadership positions.

Statement of the Problem

Findings such as these motivated the researcher's decision to conduct this study. A comprehensive search of the literature revealed that a few studies have been conducted which focused exclusively on African American women administrators (Jones, 1991). Due to a lack of research on African American women in higher education, Gill and Showell (1991) concluded that career goals, promotion, success formula, and motivation for African American women needs to be explored. Recent increases in African American women administrators at historically black institutions and traditionally white institutions compared to other groups may be the result of increased recruitment, mentoring programs or a general commitment by these institutions to increase the numbers of black females in leadership positions. Research that has been done on recruitment, retention, and promotion of African American women administrators has raised more questions than it has answered as to why more of these women are not found at both black and white institutions of higher education as administrators. This study emerged from that research milleu.

Theoretical Framework

The low number of African American women administrators in higher education raises concerns about the issues of equity. Therefore, this study draws upon research in business and industry that addresses such issues and analyzes the underlying reasons, or theoritcal causes, for inequality and inequity in employment and earning power (Simmons, 1994). These theories and resultant explanations of social phenomena in industrial organizations were used to guide the analysis of data in this study. Specifically, human capital theory is used as a theoritcial model for categorizing, analyzing and reporting the data.

Human Capital Theory

Darity (1982, 1989) looks at the problem of black/white earning inequality through a framework of human resources capital theory where he made three central assumptions: (1) labor markets are competitive and employers are animated by profit-maximizing motives; (2) black and white workers are equally productive; and (3) whites have an "externally" acquired "taste for discrimination"—a preference for hiring and working with other whites.

In his use of the human capital approach, Darity (1982) defined "human capital" as whatever characteristics an individual possesses that produces earned income. According to the human capital theorists, blacks tend to acquire or accumulate less of these earned-income producing characteristics than whites. Thus, blacks are paid less and are unemployed more frequently.

In higher education, human capital would equate to education, experience, networking, professional development, tenure, scholarly activities and prestige (Becker, 1993). Even within higher education, blacks with an enormous amount of human capital are viewed as generally less productive, which reduces the demand for blacks at the faculty and administrative levels. Blacks are also viewed as having acquired less of the traits conducive to administrative job performance (Darity, 1982).

Johnson (1991) reported the collective professional experience of women administrators coupled with previous research suggested that there is concern about the impact of certain internal and external factors (explained in detail in chapter five) on the workplace performance and career advancement of black women in community colleges. These internal and external factors can also be identified as human capital. In an effort to provide an explanation for the low numbers of black women administrators and how numbers impact the recruitment, retention, and promotion of African American women, the underlying structures of two schools of thought within the human capital framework are used in this study: (1) The Chicago School and (2) The Moynihan-Elkins School. The Chicago school places heavy emphasis on educational differences between blacks and whites. The assumption was that the quality and quantity of black education was lower than white education. Therefore, blacks were less qualified for positions of administration and, as a result, were not endowed for administrative positions. The Moynihan- Elkins School contended that black families less efficiently socialize black children for the labor market. Thus, the malfunctioning black home environment was responsible for the low human capital accumulation among African American females which could lead, consequently to the low numbers of black women administrators was a result of this flaw.

Purpose

This research was undertaken primarily to study the socialization of black females as it relates to their recruitment, retention, and promotion patterns within higher education. The study specifically focused on the equity and professional development opportunity issues surrounding the black female in higher education. Further this study increases the amount of literature in the field on black women in higher education and specifically in administrative positions.

Therefore, the two fold focus of this study was to (1) identify internal human capital factors which impact the recruitment, retention, and promotion of African American women administrators and (2) identify external human capital factors which impact recruitment, retention, and promotion patterns of African American women administrators.

Significance

This study gains its significance from the fact that few studies have focused on recruitment, retention, and promotion of black women administrators in higher education. Also this study attempts to fill theoretical gaps related to these concerns by describing the factors associated with recruitment, retention, and promotion through the framework of the Chicago School and the Moynihan-Elkins School of the human capital theory which has not been reported previously. This study describes the relationship between education and job offers; education and current employment, retention; and promotion, education and current employment, and retention promotion. The intent is that the findings reported in this exploratory study will be used to guide future researchers in studying the employment, retention and promotion of African American women administrators. This research, which has the working title, *A Descriptive Study of African American Women Administrators in Higher Education: Recruitment, Retention, and Promotion Patternss* will examine various factors (internal and external) associated with recruitment patterns, retention and promotion trends among African American women administrators within HBIs and TWIs. A consequence and personal motivation of the study is to determine whether being educated and/or employed at an HBI or TWI has an impact on recruitment, retention and promotion in higher education of black females in higher education.

The impact of recruitment, retention, and promotion of African American women administrators can be viewed as a cost or benefit to higher education. Typical cost categories include the inability of HBIs to maintain their historical significance to African American culture and the larger society. Frequent turnover in administration decreases potential for institution growth. With so few black women in higher education, HBIs are not able to compete with TWIs for potential black women administrators. HBIs cannot offer the salaries, locations, fringe benefits or accommodations for administrator's spouses. The lack of minority representation at TWIs decreases the opportunity for black students to be exposed to minority leadership. Research has shown that black students on TWI campuses without black leaders do poorly in school and some even drop out.

Potential benefits from the present research include an increase in minority representation at some institutions which appear to serve the overall black community. Turnover in administrators can bring new ideas and the opportunity for career advancement. The cost and benefits of increasing the number of African American administrators should be noted by higher education. Alexander and Scott (1983) identified the need to research "career progression of black female administrators in predominantly white institutions," many years prior to this researcher's decision to do this type of study. Alexander and Scott (1983) believe that, "Black women who will make it in academe will have to use specific strategies for coping and advancing career goals in an environment that is not quite like any other environment" (p. 6). Alexander and Scott (1983) expressed these thoughts more than 10 years ago, and they remain relevant today. Higher education is not a friendly environment to African American women. These women must create their own support networks in order to advance in such antagonistic settings. What does this mean for the future of higher education and HBIs and TWIs? Also what does it mean for the recruitment, retention, and promotion of African American women administrators? Studies such as this may provide answers to a phenomenon that is at the forefront of higher education.

Assumptions and Initial Expectations

The researcher entered this exploration with several assumptions about African American women's recruitment, retention, and promotion patterns derived from current literature in the field, focus groups, and personal interviews. From the previous existing literature, the researcher assumed the majority of highly educated African American women are employed in black colleges and universities with education being the leading field of concentration (Tobin, 1981). Since the focus of the study was on HBIs and TWIs, the researcher expected the task of finding and identifying African American female administrators at white colleges and universities to be difficult at best (Hoskins, 1978). Also, Harvard's (1986) statement that little is known about African American females and their career development, successful leadership strategies, and locations within white academic colleges and universities, caused the researcher to be doubtful about the amount of feedback that would be received from administrators.

Prior research of black women administrators indicated that they are employed on black campuses and are generally concentrated at the lower administrative level (below dean) (Moses, 1989). Moses (1989) studied black women in black institutions and found that there are fewer women in the top administrative positions in HBIs than at white institutions. Also Johnson (1991) indicated that their educational training was more positive in affecting the administrators' workplace performance than their opportunities for career advancement. Via focus group and through interviews, African American women administrators raised issues such as mentoring, African American women participation in the recruitment process, institutional involvement in the recruitment, retention, and promotion of minorities, relocation of family, isolation, additional responsibilities, administrative power, counseling, feelings about work, budget management, campus environment, number of individuals supervised, professional organizations, community involvement and affirmative action.

Therefore, the researcher relied upon the previous assumptions (focus groups and personal interviews) to guide the research, and in the end, to lead to a more comprehensive picture of the black woman administrator.

Guiding Questions

Three guiding questions were used for conducting the study. These questions included: (1) What is the possible relationship between where the administrator obtained her education (bachelor's degree and doctorate degree) and the number of job offers after completion of each degree? (2) What is the relationship between where the administrator is presently employed and her opportunity for retention and promotion? (3) What is the relationship between where the administrator obtained her education and its impact on the current employment, retention, and promotion?

Methodology

Research Subjects

The researcher selected a sample of African American women administrators that is an approximate microcosm of the working population. The sample consisted of presidents, vice presidents, provosts and deans at traditionally white institutions and historically black institutions (with and without faculty tenure). The selection of administrators was made from 117 historically black institutions and approximately 2800 traditionally white institutions, two-and four-year colleges and universities (both private and public).

Research Design

An exploratory and descriptive study using survey research was found to be appropriate for this examination of African American women administrators in higher education. Exploratory studies are useful in gaining initial insights about a particular phenomenon when a new interest is being examined or when the subject itself is new or unstudied (Babbie, 1990; Denzin 1970, 1994). Such studies generally serve three purposes: 1) to increase the researcher's understanding of the topic, 2) to test the feasibility of pursuing a more detailed study, and 3) to pilot the use of research for a more comprehensive study (Babbie, 1990).

This exploration was conducted using both quantitative (survey) and qualitative (descriptive) methods. This approach served to enhance the exploratory nature of the study and to also increase the reader's understanding of the data analysis. Qualitative research methods including observation, interview, and document analyses, are characterized by empirical practices that are sensitive to the individual's perspectives of reality (Traudt, 1981). Lofland and Lofland (1984, 1993) refer to this type of study as qualitative social research. They outline it as the processes of research that used "the data collection techniques of participant observation and/or intensive interviewing and data analysis techniques that are nonquantitative" (p. 1). The quantitative aspects of the study centered around a survey for data collection. Quantitative research measures variables which give the impression that the measure is discrete rather than continuous (Hinkle; Wiersma; & Jurs, 1988). For example, experience can take on any value on the measurement scale and is, therefore, considered a quantitative variable.

The Survey

The survey instrument was developed from preliminary discussions with black women administrators as well as an examination of existing survey instruments. First, according to Rea (1992), preliminary discussions are one of the most important sources of survey research. These discussions can provide important insights as well as firsthand knowledge of the history and current conditions of these women.

The following existing instruments were used as guides for developing the survey:

1) Alexander and Scott (1983) Factors Questionnaire on Attitude, Image, Competence, Career Mapping and Contacts.
2) Gill and Showell (1991) Survey Questionnaire on the Role of the Institution in Promoting the Ascension of African American women.
3) Konrad and Pfeffer (1991) College and University Personnel Association's Annual Administrative Compensation Survey.
4) K. Moore (1981) Leaders in Transition Survey developed by The Center for the Study of Higher Education at Penn State.
5) 1977 Administrative Compensation Survey on Employment Patterns and Salary Comparison.
6) CUPA Annual Administrative Compensation Survey.
7) 1991 Johnson Survey of Factors Affecting Workplace Performance.

Pretest

A pretest phase followed the development of the instrument which allowed for identification of poorly worded questions. The pretest afforded the researcher an opportunity to redesign the survey, as necessary. The pretest was conducted in conditions as close to the actual environment as possible. For example, the mail-out survey on African American women administrators was pretested on prior female administrators at the University of Louisville. Rea (1992) states that one or more pretests of the entire instrument should be conducted. Therefore, female administrators at other institutions in Kentucky were involved in pretesting. The researcher also was cognizant of the fact that pretests added to the time and cost of the original study.

Study Implementation

Following the pretest, the questionnaire was fine-tuned and made ready for the actual implementation process. The selected sample of African American women administrators (presidents, vice presidents, provosts, and deans of the selected schools) received letters explaining the purpose of the survey and requesting for their cooperation in completion of the survey. The purpose of the survey was to obtain information on recruitment, retention, and promotion patterns from administrators currently in the field. Mail-out surveys were distributed to selected administrators. Identifying and locating vice presidents, provosts, and deans proved to be difficult for the researcher. The data base was generated by the researcher before distribution of the survey.

During the distribution of the survey, the researcher attempted through all possible means, to ensure privacy and minimize the inconvenience to African American women administrators. For example, the researcher did not make public any information given by respondents without their consent. Contacts with administrators were kept to a minimum. Two survey reminder cards, however, were distributed to administrators following the original mailing.

Limitations

While the focus of the study involves historically black institutions and traditionally white institutions, no attempt will be made to identify or assess the quality of the institutions under study. Both private and public institutions were surveyed due to the small number of black women in administrative positions at both institutions. The exploration compared recruitment, retention, and promotion patterns of black women administrators at the historically black institutions and traditionally white institutions. The results reported in this study, while helpful in providing a better understanding of the issues confronting black women in higher education, should be approached with caution in any attempt to generalize to all African American women administrators, other women administrators, African American students, faculty, or staff.

In conducting research on African American women administrators in higher education, young social scientists should be forewarned: not all administrative staff will be cooperative with the study (Babbie, 1990).

The researcher had difficulty in obtaining a listing of African American women administrators. After the researcher received a listing of subjects, several surveys were returned because of incorrect addresses, and incorrect position classification. Also, the researcher provided "free" prints to those respondents completing the survey, and the final response rate was less than the researcher anticipated. A response rate of at least 50 percent is generally considered adequate for analysis and reporting (Babbie, 1990). The greater the response rate, the greater the ability to generalize to the larger population. This study produced a response rate of 51 percent. Generalizing from exploratory and descriptive research is extremely limited. While examinations such as this one are necessary prerequisites to more advanced comprehensive studies, this study was limited by the lack of theory in the field. Therefore, the researcher had to borrow theories from human resource management (Darity, 1982) and industrial and labor relations (Fosu, 1992). Both Darity (1982, 1989) and Fosu (1992) used the human capital approach to frame their analysis. The human capital approach (explained earlier), although used by previous researchers, has several limitations: (1) black education is viewed as being lower than white education; (2) black families ineffectively socialize their children for the market; and (3) blacks are viewed as less productive. Therefore, it is imperative that African American women in higher education continue to conduct their own research on women and people of color, and to encourage and assist the efforts of others in this exploration.

Data Analysis

The information from respondents was analyzed using the Statistical Package for the Social Sciences. Further understanding of the data was achieved by use of the Chi-square tabulations and the Elaboration Model of Multivariate Analysis appropriate to social research. The elaboration model allows for the observation of a relationship between two variables while a third variable is held constant (Babbie, 1990).

A theoretical framework based on human capital theories of human resource management and industrial and labor relations was used for organizing and analyzing qualitative data, information, about the recruitment, retention, and promotion of the research subjects.

Summary

Chapter one presented the significance of the study, the theoretical framework in which the study was designed, and problems associated with shortages of African American women in higher education. The researcher's professional and personal experiences which led to this research were expressed along with essential questions for the study, methodology, limitations, and research design. Chapter two, review of literature section addresses, the history of African American women in higher education, administration, shortages, human capital theory, and identification of the problems with recruitment, retention, and promotion of these women.

Chapter three, the methodology section, describes the qualitative and quantitative research methods used including: (a) the sample studied, (b) the survey instrument and approach used, (c) difficulties in conducting this kind of research, and (d) the survey format.

The final three chapters report and analyze the data gathered on African American women administrators in higher education (description, and data presentation). Conclusions and implications for future research are addressed in the final chapter.

Chapter II

REVIEW OF LITERATURE

Introduction

This review of literature focuses on African American women in higher education, specifically those in administrative positions. It examines related literature on the historical perspectives of African American women in higher education, the present status of African American women in higher education, the present status of African American women in higher education administration, and shortages of African American women administrators in higher education. Problems associated with the recruitment, retention, and promotion of African American women in higher education are analyzed through the human capital theory. Given the fact that very little research has been done in this area, this review is sparse.

A Brief History of African American Women in Higher Education

One hundred and sixty-seven years have passed since college education became a reality for women. In early America, the precedent for women in higher education did not exist. Chamberlain (1988) found that women first gained entry to institutions of higher education in the United States when Oberlin College admitted female students in 1837-- more than 200 years after Harvard College, the first college for men, was founded.

There are documented accounts of the historical beginnings for women in higher education. However, these beginnings are not the same for all women in higher education. African American women were introduced to higher education by white families. The early beginnings of education for African American women was highly dependent upon the educational opportunities for African American men and white women. The earliest kind of education favored the house slaves—many of them African American women (Noble, 1956). By being considered somewhat of the white master's family, these house slaves adopted behaviors and thinking similar to the white world; foreign to field slaves. Two social structures stand out as contributing to the provision of higher education for African American woman: her status as a concubine, and her role as head of the African American family (Noble, 1956). These structures appeared to elevate her position in society (Noble, 1956).

Noble (1956) states that African American women were encouraged by the *Women's Seminary Movement* among white women to build a first rate teachers college for African American women, which would teach the conventional subjects of the seminaries of that day. The original founders of African American colleges (African American women) agreed that their people needed teachers. At that time, teachers were mostly women, therefore, the African Americans who were encouraged to be teachers were mostly women (Noble, 1956). African American females, in spite of many obstacles, have continually acquired advanced degrees. However, after reaching- all time national highs of close to 1,000 advanced degree recipients in 1981, the numbers have declined in recent years. The number of doctorates earned by African Americans in 1991 was 933, down by 80 over 1981 (Status Report on Minorities in Higher Education, 1992). In 1986, African American women received 61 percent of the doctorates awarded to black candidates. Since the early inception of the black college, many changes have taken place for African Americans in education. The civil rights movement made minority issues matters of public and scholarly concern. The early 1970's initiated the formal collection of data on African Americans in higher education. Current statistics show that there are more college educated African American women than men, and more African American women occupying professional positions than African American men (Chamberlain, 1988). Prior to researching the plight of African American women in administration one may want to look more in depth at these women in higher education in faculty and other administrative ranks.

However, for this study, the researcher concentrated on African American in administration in higher education.

The number of African American women administrators in higher education is not impressive. Furthermore, these black women in higher education face a climate that is not very acceptable. Moses (1989) showed both white and historically black institutions as being cool in climate towards African American women. Her study found resentment toward African American women from both white men and white women in white institutions which she attributes to their negative reactions to affirmative action mandates. Further, Moses (1989) found that African American women and men were perceived or stereotyped as being less qualified and that they were treated with disrespect by their white colleagues. She reported that African American women in both types of institutions were treated superficially and viewed in terms of their gender orientation, that they were perceived as having a lack of status and power.

In her report of a more recent study Johnson (1991) indicated that skin color had a negative impact on workplace performance and career advancement. Although Abney and Richey (1991) studied African American women athletic administrators, the information on the discrimination experienced by these women can be generalized to women in other areas within higher education. Recent statistics on the recruitment, and retention of minorities in higher education, both as faculty members and as administrators, also reveal some progress. Slight increases in minority presidents are apparent in 1993 (178 African Americans, 54 Hispanics, 15 Asians, and 15 Native Americans) hold administrative positions in today's institutions of higher education, according to the 1993 American Council on Education Ethnicity Listing. One possible reason for more African American women than men being in administration may be what Reginald Wilson (1987), of the American Council of Education, identifies as "the decision of faculty in selecting their peers" (p. 3). That is, when identifying people to be their academic peers, white males appear to select African American females over African American males. Foster and Wilson (1942) reported from their study of women after college, that women are accepted into institutions of education designed for men, with the intent to tolerate them as long as they are not threatening to the social or academic status of male students. This same phenomenon may also exist in career ranks.

African American Administrator Shortages

In the United States in 1990, there were 25 collegiate chief executive officers who were black women (Jones, 1990). Today the number stands at 26. White women administrators comprise 298 of the Chief Executive Officers. To put that number into perspective, there are approximately 3,000 colleges and universities, and 324 women are presidents (Office of Women in Higher Education, 1993).

Moses (1989) found that there are fewer African American women in black institutions in top administrative positions than in traditionally white institutions. Williams (1986), in her study of Chief Academic Offices (CAOs) of private and public black colleges and universities, found that chief academic officers were generally held by middle-aged black males. With the majority of administrative positions being held by African American men in public black colleges and universities, African American women have yet to make an impact in higher education administration. The present numbers of African American women in administrative positions in higher education id discouraging. Historically black institutions (HBIs) hire only 10% of female administrators while traditionally white institutions (TWIs) have a slightly larger representation of African American women.

The 1992 American Council on Education Report, stated that since 1975,, the number of women administrators have grown from 9% to 14%. The reasons for such low numbers in the recruitment and retention of African American women administrators at both HBIs and TWIs are varied and complex. Another reason for the low numbers is the fact that many administrators are employed at predominantly white institutions in white communities.

Problems associated with an education pipeline devoid of African American participants have been the subject of numbers articles within the education community (Darling-Hammond, 1984: Garibaldi, 1988, Graham, 1987; Irvine, 1988: Kunjufu, 1982-90: and Witt, 1982, 1988). From the various explanations, a common thread has emerged in the process of reviewing factors contributing to African American administrator shortages. According to Tack and Patitu (1992), current trends: including low faculty salaries, few women and minorities in education pipeline, and low current job satisfaction suggest an impending shortage of willing and able women and minority candidates.

In the next century and continuing for many decades, a serious shortage will exist of people to fill vacant administrator positions, with women and minorities obviously underrepresented in a number of levels of management. Only a small number of African American women are now in the academic pipeline, and most of these women who complete the doctorate often choose other forms of employment because they do not perceive higher education administration as viable career choice.

Mazon and Ross (1990) reported data suggesting that only a small number of college graduates in general continue along the pipeline to graduate and continue on to professional schools after completing the bachelor's degree. Earlier research addressed factors that contributed to the empty pipeline that focused on increased employment opportunities, declining interest in higher education, and decreased financial aid. To date, articles can be found that continue to address the lack of African American women in leadership positions due to the above reasons.

Increased Employment Opportunities

One of the factors associated with the empty pipeline are increased employment opportunities. Doors were opened by civil rights advocates for African Americans to study in fields other than teaching and social work. There is competition from many college to attract a large portion of the small number of African American students who do attend college. Over 30,000 degrees were awarded to minorities in medicine, law, engineering, and other professions in 1985. In that year, only 3,400 degrees in education went to African American (Alston, 1988). Since 1975, the relative number of minorities earning doctoral degrees has increased while the number of white earning Ph.D.s declined (Mazon & Ross, 1990). Progress is being made in the recruitment opportunities area, and junior, as well as mid-managers, are being encouraged by mentors to move up the ladder into executive administrative positions. Institutions of higher education have begun to establish comprehensive campaigns targeted at diversifying and increasing administrative positions through appropriate publications, public relations programs, followed up by written acknowledgments, personalized calls or interviews. Several colleges and universities have established minority vitae banks in order to identify and attract African Americans.

Declined Interest in Higher Education

In addition to an increase in outside education opportunities available to African Americans there is a decline in the number of African

Americans entering college. For African American students, the African American administrator shortage begins in high school and continues its downward trend into two and four year colleges, on into professional and graduate schools. The traditionally low numbers of African American entering college has become a noted issue for graduate education. The problem is exacerbated by the fact that 82% of the minority college graduates go directly into the civilian labor force (Mazon & Ross, 1990). One known fact is that minority bachelor degree graduates in the pipeline are found in business and education, fields with a large labor force of participation by minorities. Higher education is unable to attract these minorities. The gateway to graduate school for African American deciding to engage in studies beyond the bachelor's degree begins with serious motivation issues.

Brown's (1987) findings indicate that African American youth have little interest in higher education, seeing no great advantage in working toward a degree nor having one. Increased numbers of minority students are selecting vocational-technical schools and the military over college. Minorities make up 32 percent of the enrollment in proprietary, business and technical schools (Mazon & Ross, 1990).

More and more African American students are being encouraged to attend urban community colleges that admit large numbers of students who have not been well prepared academically and require remediation. As a consequence, fewer of these students earn bachelor's degree and less enter graduate professional schools.

Decreased Financial Aid

The third factor to African American administrator shortages is a decrease in financial aid available to students. Institutions of higher education throughout the country have developed several programs to assist minorities with the financial burden of their graduate studies. Such programs basically include offering fellowships and assistantships to attract and maintain minority students. African American college enrollments peaked in the early 1980s and then began to decline due to decreased financial aid available in the form of grants and low interest loans Mazon & Ross, 1990). Reduced financial aid in succeeding years caused African American students to be unable to meet the costs of tuition and forced them to turn to loans or give up graduate school. Also, African American students are frequently unaware of the various types of financial aid available. Therefore, their decision to go further with their education is based upon incomplete information.

Recruitment of African American Women Administrators

Due to a recognition of obvious shortages at ethnic and cultural diversity, and the effects of racism, and sexism which have plagued the career development of black females, recent commitments of institutions of higher education has been to diversity staff profiles by hiring and promoting various minority group members and women. While we tend to assume good faith efforts and real progress go together, conclusive data are rarely produced to support results from initiatives to diversity the administrative ranks in higher education (Harter, Moden, & Wilson, 1989). While there is some evidence of progress over the last ten years, there is also evidence of an insidious attempt to limit the black female's progress above and barriers which prevent black females from obtaining top leadership roles in higher education (Gill & Showell, 1991). Konrad and Pfeffer (1991), in their study on hiring of women and minorities in educational institutions, found women and minorities were significantly more likely to be hired for jobs, organizations, and positions held by members of their own group in the past. The number of women in particular jobs across the institution, the number of women in administrative positions and the fact that the predecessor was a woman all had a positive unique effect on the odds that a new hire was a woman. The same effects of minority composition on hiring of minorities were similar. Konrad & Pfeffer (1991) hypothesized that women and minorities would be ore likely to be promoted from within than hired from outside the organization. To counteract attempts to undermine the progression of black women in higher education aggressive programs have been designed and implemented to recruit minorities and women into administration. For example, Baker (1991), reported that the University of California-Berkeley Chancellor recruits candidates to administrative positions through a nationwide search for minorities seeking post-doctoral training. In the spirit of the "grow your own" concept, (Baker, 1991) Washington University in St. Louis and, to a limited degree, Wayne State University, in Detroit, aggressively recruit in disciplines where minorities are grossly underrepresented.

Institutions over the years have attempted to increase the increase the presence of African American women on their college campuses. However, these methods have been very successful (Willie & others, 1991). Willie, Grady, and Hope (1991) conclude that recruitment efforts should probably differ from the recruitment methods for whites because of the small pool of applicants. Some feel that institutions must further expand their efforts for recruiting, retaining and promotions of African American women in higher education.

Retention of African American Women Administrators

The commitment of institutions to recruit and promote minority groups and women is not supported through a review of the retention patterns of these individuals in higher education. Mercer (1992) found leadership changes so frequently that observers wonder if there is a "revolving door" in the president's office at historically black institutions (HBIs). HBI presidents (male and female) have commented that, when they ponder the future of the institutions, one of their most pressing concerns is turnover. Whether the turnover phenomenon is worse in HBIs than in TWIs many agree that even if the rates are the same, the effects on HBIs are more harmful, due to the fact that HBIs are smaller, have fewer resources, and demand more from their administrators.

Dr. Herman Black (1992), former president of Tougaloo College, surveyed HBI presidents and board members and found that these schools are changing presidents every three or four years; therefore, the administrative staying power that may be required to allow institutions to grow and advance is thus lost. Dr. Herman B. Smith (1992), former president of the University of Arkansas-Pine Bluff and now interim president of Jackson State University, believes the short-time syndrome is not a HBI phenomenon, but a higher education phenomenon. Other black presidents (male and female) not only see the revolving door as a higher education problem, but a problem of perception on the part of the new administrator (Mercer, 1992). Dr. Prezell Robinson (1992), St. Augustine College, stated part of the retention problem at HBIs is that young black college presidents (male and female) come into the job with the notion that it is a glorious. prestiges position.

Institutions of higher education have fallen short in attracting and retaining minority faculty and staff. Retention problems perhaps contributed to Affirmative Actions programs which have not significantly increased the participation of minorities in predominantly white colleges and universities. Because administrators and faculty members lack commitment to racial balance, and because of weak enforcement of Affirmative action regulations by the federal government. Other reasons for retention problems of African American women is institutionalized discriminatory practices which prevent minorities from recruitment and retention as well as promotion opportunities. Many African American women are nominated for positions but are never actually placed in the position; resulting in these women going elsewhere for positions.

Many educators have said to substantially increase participation of minority students, faculty, and staff, new policies and strategies aimed at long-term recruitment and retention need to be developed and implemented at all levels of the university structure. High education's survival depends upon the ability of its educational institutions to increase and maintain active representation of African American women administrators on their campuses. Higher education in this country can no longer afford the luxury of catering to the few and must assume active responsibility for retaining African American women and men.

The institution's president must ensure that African American women are not only recruited into entry level positions at their institution but are also maintained and encouraged for upper level administrative positions. Departments should also have plans to ensure African American women faculty are given the opportunity to participate as an administrator and to move toward a tenured position.

Minority involvement is especially crucial in retention efforts of African American women. Research has shown that networking is extremely useful in recruiting and retaining minorities. Networking appears to be found in liberal arts and two-year or community colleges. Phillip (1993) found within a four year institution, the largest number of women are retained at liberal arts institutions, while male administrators are found more often in comprehensive colleges and universities. Women presidents are more likely to be found in two-year and community colleges in urban settings (Phillip, 1993).

Promotion of African American Women Administrators in Higher Education

The frequent turnover among administrators can cripple the black female when promotion opportunities arise. Female, as well as male, college presidents need to be more sensitive to the relevant issues in promotion of African American women. The African American female may have the privilege of being a faculty member and/or holding lower level traditional administrative positions, better opportunities for promotion are slim and may not exist in many instances.

In a survey conducted with African American female administrators, the rates of promotions for ten African American females at Bowie State University (1989), ten reported no promotions, seven reported one promotion, three reported four promotions, and two reported three promotions (Gill & Showell, 1991). However, the data indicate a number of respondents who have been at the institution longer have had the same job title over time. African American women administrators listed a number of factors they considered to be crucial to promotion opportunities: (1) experience, (2) networking, (3) politics, (4) friendships, and (5) faculty recommendations. These same women identified their supervisors as not being helpful or encouraging to their advancement.

Theoretical Framework

Introduction

A theory is a systematic, organized group of assumptions, principles or rules within which research can be conducted and analyzed. It is a formal structure for addressing issues in research. The theory of human capital, borrowed from the fields of human resource management and industrial relations, is used in this study as a theoretical framework. This study is concerned with the internal and external factors which impact the recruitment, retention, and promotion patterns of African American women administrators in high. These internal and external factors have been identified by early researchers as investment of human capital.

Definition of Human Capital

Most studies that have attempted quantitative assessments of contribution to growth have assigned an important role to investment in human capital (Becker, 1993). Human capital has been defined as investment in schooling, job training, medical care, migration, searching for information, the virtues of punctuality and honesty. A more detailed listing and description of these investments will be explained later in this chapter.

History of Human Capital

What has been called the human capital "revolution" began about three decades ago. Its pioneers include Ted Schultz, Jacob Mincer, Milton Friedman, Sherwin Rosen, and several others associated with the University of Chicago (Becker, 1993). The past decade has witnessed intensive concern with and research on the investment in human capital, much of it begun or formulated by T.W. Schultz. The theory of human has been with us now for more than three decade during which time the amount of literature in the field was steadily grown and seems to be increasing at a rapid rate. Three American Scholars—Jacob Mincer, Gary Becker and Therodore Shultz—revived an age-old idea that education is a process whereby individuals accumulate "human capital" (Baugh, 1992). The idea of human capital easily arouses passions on the subject and some people who are advocates of education, medical care, and the like often dislike the phrase "human capital" and doubt its role in the economics of our society. The attention paid to the economic effects of education and other human capital in this study is not in anyway meant to imply that other effects are unimportant or less important than economic ones (Becker, 1993).

In the early days of human capital, a number of people criticized the term and the underlying analysis because they believed it treated people like slaves or machines. It should also be noted that the concept of human capital remains suspect within academic circles that organize their thinking about social problems around a belief in the exploration of labor or capital (Becker, 1993).

Although the theory is suspect in academe, its general purpose has a number of important applications. As referred to earlier, the theory helps to explain such diverse phenomena as education, job training, health, migration, searching for information, punctuality, honesty, years in current position, having mentor, engaging in networking, field of study for doctorate and master's degree, socializing with non-African American administrators, belonging to a support group, doctorate degree year, undergraduate degree year, current position, employment opportunities, the number of African American female and male administrators on a campus; all of which improve health, raise earnings, or add to a person's appreception of self over much of his or her lifetime. For Schultz, Becker, and Miner human capital formation is typically conceived as being carried out by individual acting in their own interests (Baugh, 1992).

Explanations of Accumulated Human Capital

Probably the most impressive piece of evidence of the accumulation of human capital is that more highly educated, skilled persons almost always tend to earn more than others. This is true in the United States, the former Soviet Union as well as underdeveloped countries (Becker, 1993). An administrator's investment in education and training are the most popular investments in education and many other studies report college education in the United States greatly increases a person's income level after expenses have been deducted for the cost of the education.

On-the-job training is purported to be important source of very large increases in earnings as administrators gain greater work experience. Jacob Mincer (1988) suggests that the total investment in on-the-job training maybe almost as large as the investment in education.

An administrator's health as well as job training is an important aspect of their human capital. Investment in medical care health plans, membership in exercise fitness centers, and monitoring of a proper diet are all important to an administrators investing in self-worth and interest (Becker, 1993).

It appears that job changes or migration from one job site to another can be identified as human capital accumulation. In Japan, job changes are less frequent than in the United States, due to the fact that on-the-job training and education investment in workers are greater in Japan than the United States.

Before migrating to various job locations, administrators normally search for information on their new location. This process to search for information cab be identified as an invaluable form of accumulation of physical capital. Through their search, the administrator learns of other areas of interest, storing this newly learned information as a resource to be used later (Becker, 1993).

In their search for information, administrators need also be concerned with punctuality and the honesty of their actions. These factors also contribute to the administrator's accumulation of human capital. Many employers value an employee who is punctual and honest. This human capital factor can very easily lead to possibilities of promotion and additional income.

The number of years an administrator has been in their present position as well as their punctuality and honesty can also increase the value of their human capital. Administrators that have accumulated several years in their present position generally can expect to be considered for a promotion or an increase in pay.

The fact that an administrator has been in their present position for a number of years could be attributed to having had a mentor who provided support and valuable information to the administrator. Mentors can assist administrators in providing valuable information on their personal and professional surroundings as well as opportunities for advancement.

Networking coupled with mentoring can be a very important tool to an administrator when an opportunity arises for the possibility of promotion or migration. African American are not known for utilizing networking in the same sense as their white counterparts. Increasing networking skills (acquiring professional and personal contacts which provide information to the administrator) definitely can result in an increase in human capital.

The field of study in which an administrator obtained an education may have been influenced by a mentor or due to their networking contacts. The majority of African Americans have selected education as a primary field of study and excelled in this area for the last 200 years. Therefore, the amount of human capital invested in education by this group is enormous.

The amount of socialization of African Americans with non-African Americans may differ by field of study. For example, if the non-African American has chosen a field of study of education, African American may socialize with this individual on a more frequent basis than if this field of study was biology. Socialization with non-African Americans outside the workplace could be a tool used to increase human capital.

Socialization with non-African Americans outside of work may or may not be affected by the fact that the administrator belongs to a support group for African American faculty and staff. A support group can provide a tremendous amount of information and critical feedback in a supportive environment. They type of support to which an administrator may belong can be an additional source of human capital (e.g. sorority, church, community service or organizations).

The year an administrator received her undergraduate or doctoral degree could have resulted in an increase in their human capital. During the 1980s, increasing the educational level of a worker was rewarded through increased job opportunities, possibility for promotion and an increase in salary. Today, workers are rewarded for both, requiring additional skills and education.

An administrator's current position may have been made possible simply because the administrator obtained additional education. The current position title has the possibility of increasing the administrator's human capital because of the prestige, status or power attached to the position.

The number of employment opportunities available after completion of an undergraduate or doctoral degree could be directly related to the amount of human capital the administrator has acquired. Employment opportunities are defined as the number of times an administrator has been involved in the recruitment process in higher education.

The number of employment opportunities may depend upon the number of African American male of female administrators on campus, and may be a factor in other African Americans joining the faculty and staff of that particular campus. The number of male or female African American administrators on campus could be related to socialization, support groups or networking.

The list of human capital is exhaustive. The factors discussed above are human, not physical or financial capital.

The administrator cannot separate her knowledge, skills, abilities, health, or values in the way it is possible to move financial and physical assets while the owner stays put.

Research on Human Capital

As with prior researcher's the theoretical framework for this study was adopted from the field of business and industry. It might be said, with justification, that the modern analysis of (primarily) the inequality of black and white earnings differences began with Gary Becker's, *The Economics of Discrimination*, published in 1957 (Darity, 1982). However, in time, this pure labor market discrimination approach was not sufficient in terms of its internal logic to attempt to justify the existence of wage differences between equally qualified and productive workers.

Becker (1957, 1978) first assumed that imperfect competition could be introduced by positing either (1) that some firms have monopoly in the product market and these firms prefer to hire white workers, (Monopolists may have more incentive to hire for other reasons than performance), (2) that white laborers have monopoly position in some labor markets. (Once positioned in the more profitable sectors of the economy, white laborers can prevent African Americans from competing with them for jobs.); (3) that there is racially uneven access to financial capital; (flat refusal of whites to hire African Americans). Inequality is thus said to e rooted in the lack of African American acquired human capital. This could easily be the case in institutions of higher education. Reynolds (1979) points out, the firms that are monopolists may have greater discretion in hiring labor on grounds other than performance. Monopoly firms where management is opposed to African Americans could choose to hire only whites. This may be the situation of hiring among many TWIs and HBIs. Some TWIs are hiring to increase minority representation on their campuses, and HBIs may hire to maintain cultural identity.

Anne Krueger (1963), in her adaptation of Becker's original model, say that white capitalists restricted black access to financing. In this explanation, white capitalists strive to maximize white workers incomes rather than their own. This theory may also be operating in the halls of higher education, and especially in the administrative ranks of these institutions.

Two basic arguments have resulted from the assumption that wage differences that do not need to resort to less than perfect competition: (1) African Americans and whites have the same level of productivity, but African Americans have a higher range of abilities. Therefore, what is known as "statistical" discrimination occurs even when African American and whites have the same capabilities. Also, African Americans and whites are perceived as having the same level of abilities, but employers identify job potentials by the use of placement list. Aptitude tests or intelligence test are not good at predicting African American ability.

In reviewing racial wage differentials, economists (Darity, 1982) revised Becker's original assumption that African Americans and whites have the same abilities. This step produced the ingredients of the human capital approach to African American- white earnings inequality. African Americans, in this theory, are classified as being "less productive" than whites. Therefore, the logic is that African American can reasonably be expected to be paid less and to be promoted or advanced into administrative ranks in fewer numbers.

Usages of Human Capital Theory

Tack and Patitu (1992) reported that until relatively recently, most research about job satisfaction was completed in the industrial sector, with attempts often made to adapt findings to higher education. In their research efforts, these researchers borrowed internal and external factors from the business sector that lead to job satisfaction.

Fosu (1992), in his analysis of occupational mobility of black women, used individual characteristics (internal factors) and institutional factors (external factors) to describe the occupational distribution of African American women. Individual characteristics such as education, race and gender were describe as human capital factors. Institutional factors were those characteristics connected to supply demand conditions of the labor market. Fosu (1992) concluded that the observed increase in African American female, upward-occupational mobility after 1964, appears not to be influenced by either individual characteristics or institutional factors.

Schools of Human Capital Theory

Two schools of though are used to expound upon the human capital approach (differences among African American and white human capital accumulation). First, The Chicago School assumes that the type of education African Americans received is inferior to that of whites. Smith and Welch (1975) points to evidence on lower number of days of school attended and lower numbers of grades completed by African American to produce poorer quality of African American education, although this may have been offset by more committed teachers and the deep sense of struggle among southern black communities faced at the time. The second school of Moynihan-Elkins basically espouse the theory that African Americans families were not properly functioning in society and, therefore, produced children that were malfunctioning in society. The proof usually given is the large number of African American female-headed families. This malfunction in the African American home is supposedly the reason for the alleged racial differences in human capital among African Americans and whites.

Arleen Leibowitz (1974) concludes the view that the crucial phase of human capital accumulation occurs in the home during childhood. In his practical application, Thomas Sowell (1971) asserts that the cultural experiences of African American people black the development of the kinds of behavior characteristics and attitudes conducive to high productivity performance on the job:

> The pattern of cumulative inequalities in human capital investment is repeated in the other forms of human capital. The whole way of thinking and behaving appropriate to the more lucrative and responsible occupations is something which comes freely, and even unconsciously,

to people reared in families where such occupations have been common for generations, where-as human capital comes to the low-income person only slowly, imperfectly and with great deliberate efforts to break his natural pattern. Such basic traits as punctuality, efficiency and long-run planning are little use to people who have been limited to menial jobs for generations as with most African Americans. Everyone can understand the economic value of such traits as an abstract intellectual proposition but to understand such qualities abstractly and to have such *habits* in reality are very different things. Those African Americans people who have such traits have typically acquired them through persistent and sometimes painful adjustments, which would be difficult to explain to people who grew up with those patterns as a free cultural inheritance (p. 7).

Freeman (1964), who places a heavy emphasis on family background characteristics as the sources of remaining earnings differences, has used longitudinal data to measure the relationship between family background characteristics and years of schooling. He found that 70 percent of the differences for adult men and 80 percent of the differences for adolescent boys in years of schooling are left unexplained. Therefore, an accumulation of family background malfunctioning may not account for the differences in socialization of African Americans in families.

There is no question that family has an impact on individual personal development, and this probably influences one's performance in higher education. Certain types of environments a person is exposed to in childhood may be more conducive to "success" than others in capitalist society or mainstream society.

In their presentation on how society reproduces social stultification, Bowles and Gentis (1975), focused on the non- cognitive attributes children acquire from their families (and the schools) that are desired by employers. In effect, Bowels (1972) conclusions amount to basically the same cause and effect chain that Moynihan-Elkins espouse on inequality initiating from the home to the labor market (higher education).

Darity (1982) shows that the self-investment notion portrays individuals as choosing additional education and training in anticipation of a higher stream of lifetime earnings. This demands individuals aspiring to be administrators to have sufficient knowledge of career possibilities and the future of higher education. They must be able to calculate certain equivalent for the amount of return on their education and job performance investment and to act as if they have made such calculation. In other words, if obtaining a doctorate degree in higher education administration is your goal then you should set your educational preparation and personal energies to fulfil this goal.

In contrast to the prior theories of quality of education and maladapted family backgrounds Leigh and Rawlins (1974) attempted to control for various productivity—related characteristics. Their investigation revealed that the largest proportion of the differences is explained solely by race. Racial unemployment differentials are emphasized even more in light of the Welch-Smith (1978) "vintage hypothesis." Smith and Welch (1978; 1976) have argued that the gains African Americans have made in recent years are the consequence of younger cohorts of African Americans becoming more similar to their white peers in human capital attributes.

In actuality, acquiring additional human capital (e.g. education) still does not guarantee African Americans a place in employment market today. Robert Hill (1979) has observed: While almost no one would deny that higher educational attainment increases one's employment opportunities, such a relationship fails to hold when one compares the unemployment patterns of black youth with those of white youth with similar or lower educational levels (p. 3).

The modern development of this approach is largely attributed to the work of Peter Doeringer and Michael Piore (1972) borrowing heavily from the tradition of labor market analysts who concerned themselves with the institutional processes guiding the information of contracts between management and labor. Doeringer and Piore (1972) conceived of the labor market as being comprised of two sections—a primary sector with stable and well-paid jobs and a secondary sector with high turnover and low paid jobs (Darity, 1982). Higher education has a similar labor market of professors and administrators and within these levels are the tenured versus untenured and lower entry level versus executive level.

Another researcher shares Doeringer and Piore (1972) views on the existence of a dual system of the labor market. Jill Rubery (1978) points out, neoclassical economists have also explained the existence of dual or segmented markets for black and white labor; leading them directly to their own theories of internal labor markets.

Piore (1972) himself has argued that there is a feedback loop from the socialization of black and white youths to their productivity characteristics to the preferences of employers that operates to locate a larger fraction of blacks in secondary employment. The cultural experiences of whites allegedly make them better suited for administrative type of positions, while the cultural experiences of blacks supposedly prepare them for the lower level mid-managers positions. Basically, the white home environment in which most white youth are reared is assumed to be more stable. Thus, coinciding with the stable primary job sector (e.g. presidents, vice presidents, ceo's and others). Therefore, African American youth are supposedly reared in an unstable home environment which predisposes them toward unstable careers in the secondary sector (e.g. blue collar workers, plant managers, program coordinators and others).

Ray Marshall, too has sought to explain why blacks are located disproportionate in particular sectors of the economic structure in a more institutional vein. He basically believes that blacks generally have lower levels of skill than whites. Marshall (1974) attaches great importance to strict racial discrimination by setting aside the neoclassical theories of internal labor markets and focusing on what he describes as the greater bargaining power of white labor over black labor into theory he factors exclusionary practices of white unions.

Darity (1982) purports that the human capital approach simply does not stand up well against the facts it purports to explain— racial income inequality. However, the human capital approach is not used in this study to prove or disprove a hypothesis. It is simply used to frame the data analysis of an exploration into a topic lacking in present theoretical guidelines.

Summary

This chapter presented a literature review of several areas of interest on African American women administrators: historical points in education, administrative positions, shortages of African Americans in higher education, increase in employment opportunities for these women, decline interest in higher education among African Americans, decrease in financial aid to minorities, theoretical framework (human capital approach), black and white inequality, and recruitment, retention and promotion patterns of African American women.

Chapter III

Methodology

Research Approach and Rationale

This research project was an exploratory study designed to yield descriptive data to portray the perceptions of African American women administrators' serving in the position of dean and above at institutions of higher education. The primary method of data collection was a personal-design survey that was conducted through a mail-out questionnaire. The survey approach employed a system associated with efficiency in gathering information from large numbers of participants (Simmons, 1987). The decision to study African American women in higher education administration resulted from a review of literature and encouragement from several administrators in the field. A great deal of consideration was also given to Lofland and Lofland's (1984) suggestion of "starting where you are" which was to say "using the current situation or past involvements as a research topic" (p.2).

Quantitative Method

Two types of research methods were employed in this project, quantitative and qualitative. Survey research is considered as quantitative or empirical research in sociology. A device that is most frequently used in gathering field data, especially where this survey technique is employed, is the questionnaire (Gopal, 1964). According to Gopal (1964) this technique is preferred in the United States because it allows for an easier and more convenient way of studying a representative sample.

A survey is generally a detailed, classified, planned and ordered list of items to which a response is required. Its main purpose is to obtain concrete quantitative and objective data from the subjects. Sometimes, as in this case of exploratory survey, it is used to initiate a piece of research.

Qualitative Method

Qualitative research methods were used in this study to augment the quantitative aspects of the research. Qualitative data consist of detailed descriptions of situations, events, people interactions, and observed behaviors. Direct quotations from respondents about their experiences, attitudes, beliefs, and thoughts and excepts or entire passages from documents, correspondence, records, and case histories are used to round out the data (Patton, 1980).

Erickson (1986) provides eight alternative descriptors for qualitative methods of investigative: ethnographic, qualitative, participant observation, case study, symbolic interactionist, phenomenological, constructivist, and interpretive. Palonsky (1986), states that the ethnographer focuses inquiry on the mundane, everyday practices of people in social settings. According to Simmons (187), Doyle (1979) and Bronfenbrenner (1979) round out the description with their use of the term "ecological research" in reference to this form of holistic inquiry.

Qualitative methods have been accepted largely for filling many gaps in educational research (Cusack, 1983; Doyle, 1979; Erikson, 1982; Lightfoot, 1983; Ogbu, 1978; Waller, 1932; Wolcott, 1977). It is useful to combine insights gained through qualitative research means may be combined in a useful manner with quantitative information (Erikson, 1986); Green & Harker, 1982; Green & Wallet, 1981; Sight & Pillemer, 1982). Although the majority of information in this study was obtained by using quantitative methods, the researcher utilized qualitative methods (focus group, review of documents, individual interviews, and survey pretest) to describe the perceptions of the respondents.

Definitions of Terms

African American, black, and Negro

The cultural identification and ethnic background of respondents in this study.

Administrator

Individuals identified in their current position as president, vice president, dean, director, coordinator and supervisor; supervises and coordinates programs and activities of the units as identified on the organizational chart of university administrators and may hold faculty rank and tenure.

Recruitment

A search process initiated by a faculty search committee in order to acquire additional faculty or administrators.

Retention

The amount of time an administrator has spent in a given position at an institution of higher education.

Promotion

An actual upgrade or increase in rank/level to the next available administrative rank/level.

Selecting A Topic

In researching the topic of African American women administrators, the researcher discovered that theory is virtually nonexistent in this area. Also, the availability of published information on African American women administrators in higher education is extremely limited. It became apparent that one interested in pursuing this topic must search the literature as extensively as possible before deciding on a particular focus. The researcher should begin with the use of open exploration. This perspective of gathering information is better known as triangulation. Brewer (1981) defined triangulation is a model which employs the idea that multiple vantage points permit fixing on a common object of perception in a way that is impossible from a single point. In this study, the researcher used three different perspectives in which to assist in the formation of the study: (1) focus group of African American and white women, (2) review of documentation, (4) individual interviews; and (5) survey pretest. In beginning this study of African American women administrators, this researcher was not aware of the amount of interest the topic would generate among informants and advisors. In selecting the topic, the researcher found that the subject matter would not only be a dissertation topic, but could constitute the basis for publication. Due to the limited amount of research done in this area, encouragement was given to conduct this study at all cost, regardless of the problems associated with this type of research. The researcher was totally unaware of the fact that several national organizations, colleges and universities around the nation, were interested in the topic.

Population, Sample, and Sampling Procedures

During November 1993, 301 surveys were disseminated throughout the United States for this study, to a select group of African American women administrators, identified from private and public sources, in the position of dean and higher (president, vice president, dean). African American women in other positions (director, coordinator and special assistant). participated in the study also. The mailing list of African American women administrators was developed by the researcher from information obtained from national organizations, journals, newsletters, state offices of higher education, and other researchers in the field. Forty-nine historically black institutions and 96 traditionally white institutions participated in the survey. They comprised a combination of two and four year colleges and universities, both private and public.

Research Questions

The Chicago School (quality and quantity of education of African American children) and the Mohynihan-Elkins School (socialization of African American children) of human capital theory explained earlier were used in the development of the two essential questions, and the three guiding questions. The two essential questions used to organize this study were: (1) What are the internal factors impacting recruitment, retention, and promotion of administrators? (2) What are the external factors impacting recruitment, retention, and promotion of administrators? Internal factors were: (1) currently having a mentor; (2) report of engaging in networking; (3) report of belonging in a support group; (4)

number of years of experience in higher education; and (5) educational preparation. External factors were: (1) socializing with non-African American administrators; (2) community support; (3) number of individuals supervised; (4) colored glass-ceiling; (5) present position; and (6) administrative power and responsibilities.

The three guiding questions used were: (1) What is the relationship between where an administrator received her education and the number of job offers she received after receiving her bachelor's and doctorate degrees? (2) What is the relationship between an administrators' current employment institution and number of years in current position, number of promotions in higher education, and promotions at the current institution? (3) What is the relationship between where an administrator received her education and her current employment institution, number of years in higher education, number of years in current position, promotions in higher education and promotions at the current institution? The theoretical framework, based on the two schools of human capital, was adopted from the human resource management and industrial labor and relations fields. Fosu (1992) also used the human capital approach in his investigation of occupational mobility of African American women. His approach identified human capital in terms of internal and external characteristics. Fosu's (1992) identifiers were used in this study to classify the factors possibly affecting recruitment, retention, and promotion of African American women in administration.

Data Collection

Difficulties Obtaining Information

The researcher received hundreds of letters and a number of telephone calls concerning the topic. Attempting to locate the administrators consumed much of the researcher's time and energy. Although this is a topic of personal interest, it became unmanageable at times. Contact was made with several local and national organizations and other researchers in the field in an effort to obtain initial information on the status of African American women administrators. Many national organizations were not be able or were unwilling to provide information. Many organizations do not maintain lists of African American women administrators in higher education and could offer no ideas on how to go about obtaining this information. Background searches, telephone calls, letters, and travel to conduct personal interviews constituted the various avenues the researcher used to obtain information for the design and initiation of the study.

The researcher spent hours on the telephone, writing letters requesting information, and reading correspondence received—only to discover the information requested was not available or the writer was hesitant about providing the information.

National organizations, colleges and universities are selective about the information released on African American women in higher education. In contacting organizations for information on African American women, the researcher was surprised when confronted by the apprehensiveness researcher encountered on the part of organizations, colleges, and universities. Individuals, organizations and institutions repeatedly asked about the researchers authority to obtain the information.

Conducting research on African American women administrators in higher education was not an easy task. The researcher distributed over a hundred letters requesting information on African American women administrators to organizations such as the American Council on Education, American Association of University Women, Office of Women in Higher Education and many others. The researcher was totally unprepared for the response received. Although getting specific data was difficult, individuals called from states that did not have any African Americans in higher education; except for athletes on the football or basketball team. Extensive phone connections were made by the researcher to several individuals about the study. Staff from various colleges called to express their disappointment in not having any African Americans or women in higher education. Telephone calls were received from individuals just wanting to talk to the researcher and ask questions about the origin of the topic. Correspondence poured in from around the country. Some of the information received from individuals and organizations was extremely helpful. Other information did not come close to addressing the request. The researcher attributed this phenomenon to a possible cautiousness on the part of the organizations.

Organizations providing information for the study requested a copy of the researcher's proposal and draft questionnaire. One organization, after receiving the information, contacted the researcher to request that "African Americans" be removed from the survey and that the survey be distributed to all women administrators in higher education. The same organization was contacted for a listing of African American women administrators in the position of dean and above. The researcher was told the organization's data base was not equipped to provide such a listing. Several organizations, after receiving the letter about the research being conducted on African American women administrators expressed interested in the topic. One organization promised financial support (paying for printing and mailing) and administrative support (addressing labels). The researcher was later informed that funding would be put on hold because of the lack of organizational policy concerning such issues. The researcher was asked to join a few of the organizations in order to receive their support and monthly newsletter on women in higher education. Organizations providing references and lists requested that their efforts be recorded as being cooperative with the research effort. The researcher was overwhelmed by such responses received from organizations. Individuals contacted the researcher to ensure that someone from their state had made contact concerning the topic. The researcher received telephone calls on weekends, early in the morning, and late at night from individuals. Information was sent by facsimile and delivered by Federal Express to the researcher.

Survey Format

Perhaps both phenomenon, number of responses to the preliminary contacts and difficulties in obtaining the desired information, were due, at least in part, to the fact that there is little formal documentation on African American women in higher education and/or the sensitive nature of the topic. The researcher attempted to obtain sample survey forms for the data collection phase of the study, but encountered difficulty in obtaining these forms; therefore, this study required the design of an original instrument.

Background information and guiding data were ferreted out from a wide variety of journal articles, books and published reports. A focus group of African American women and non- African American women in higher education administrative positions was helpful to the researcher in conceptualizing and structuring the survey.

Design of Survey Instrument

The survey instrument basically included six areas of concentration: (1) professional and personal background information, (2) professional education, (3) family concerns, (4) university concerns, and (5) recruitment, retention, and (6) promotion. The survey contained 105 questions and was 11 pages long. The survey was flexible, spread out, and uncluttered in appearance. Questions occupied no more than one line each (Rea, 1991). Babbie (1990) states that the professional-looking, long questionnaire is a printed booklet held together with a "saddle-stitch" (a staple in the spine). According to Babbie (1990), this type of questionnaire facilitates a better response rate from respondents. This researcher's survey was structured on that model. Finally, the survey was finally designed with features from previously developed instruments. It was structured to confirm information about some African American women administrator's current perceptions on the recruitment, retention, and promotion patterns in higher education. Some questions in the survey were open-ended while most questions were closed-ended and others were based on a Likert-scale format.

Survey Pretest

The pretest was used to revise the design and content of the survey. Before the survey was finalized and mailed out, the instrument was pretested using five African American women that had previously held the position of dean or above. The researcher had some difficulty in locating individuals to participate in the pre-test. After pre-testing the instrument, the researcher still did not have a mailing list of the target population. So the researcher decided to proceed with the final design and printing of the survey. The design and format of the survey was selected because the researcher wanted those receiving the survey to: 1) recognize immediately that research was being conducted in this area, 2) cause those receiving the survey to reflect upon the plight of African American women in higher education, 3) cause the respondents to be eager to complete the survey, and 4) produce a first class product that the researcher and respondent would be proud to see again. To ensure a high return rate, the researcher selected an artistic print, "Symmetry of Hearts," by Brenda Joysmith to give to respondents completing the survey.

Instrumentation

The researcher's dissertation time line called for mailing out the surveys in early November. The address labels were not received until mid-November, which caused the researcher to compete with the holiday season mailing rush. The return mailings were slow, and two survey reminder cards were sent out. Prior to the second survey reminder card, the researcher had received approximately 40% of the surveys. After mailing the second reminder card, an increase of an additional 10% response was received. A cover letter explaining the purpose of the survey (see APPENDIX B), a card to claim the complimentary artistic print, "Symmetry of Hearts," (to be completed by respondent in order to receive a free print of the survey cover [See APPENDIX C]), and the researcher's business card was all included in the survey packet. In addition a follow-up survey reminder card was sent during December 1993 and January 1994 to all survey participants (SEE APPENDIX D).

Cost of Survey

Approximately 400 surveys, cover letters, business cards, complimentary print cards, and survey reminder cards were printed. Printing and designing the survey instrument was expensive (researcher's choice) comparatively speaking. The cost of the survey was shared with an African American woman who owned her own advertising firm and was interested in the research. She had the surveys printed at a discount rate. The print "Symmetry of Hearts" was obtained wholesale through an art gallery owned by a white female who was also interested in the topic.

Three hundred and three surveys were mailed out at bulk rate from several mailing lists provided by individual researchers, organizations, and higher education journals. Approximately 145 artistic prints were mailed out the respondents completing and returning the survey.

Management and Synthesis of Data

The data were maintained in as simple a form as possible. The decision to use simple management procedures was made in an attempt to keep the researcher from being overwhelmed by the amount of data collected. After data collection the information was hand coded and then entered into the Statistical Packages for Social Science Database (SPSS-X). Surveys were kept in order by the date received and assigned a numerical number in SPSS-X. The researcher transformed raw data into the storage systems for rapid retrieval and management purposes as soon as possible (Lofland & Lofland 1984, 1993 Patton 1980, 1990).

Data Analysis & Interpretation

Data analysis took place throughout the collection process. The process of coding subjective responses (open- ended) was the initial stage of data analysis. Thus, the preliminary routine coding helped to clarify the analysis of data. The last part of analysis occurred after data collection had ceased and information had placed in SPSS-X system. This section will describe that final task.

Statistical Analysis

Data was coded into the SPSS-X system by category and by variable number. Each response was assigned a numerical number in order to transform data into machine-readable form. After the researcher had assimilated all of the data, the next step was that of analytical interpretation. The effort of "making sense" out of the collected materials in preparation for reporting it to others then began (Bogden & Biklen, 1982; Guba & Lincoln, 1985). This procedure, in turn, lead to the selection or construction of some type(s) of management and interpretative framework.

As shown in the previous section, one framework model guided the latter stages of data analysis in this exploration. This model was the human capital approach that was outlined by Darity (1982). Human capital was defined earlier as characteristics an individual possesses that produces earned income. Two schools within the human capital approach were used to frame this investigation. The Chicago School and the Monynihan-Elkins School (Darity, 1982). Fosu (1992) also used the human capital approach in his investigation of occupational mobility of African American women. His approach identified human capital in terms of internal and external characteristics. Fosu's (1992) identifiers were used in this study to classify the factors possibly effecting recruitment, retention, and promotion of African American women in administrators. The final stage of the study involved actually writing the descriptions and statistical analyses of the survey data. The descriptions found in chapter four, included basic demographic information and the respondent's attitudes expressed about their current position (e.g. how do you feel about working at your current institution). The statistical analyses found in chapter five included cross-tabulations used to identify the impact certain internal and external factors may have had an impact on the recruitment, retention, and promotion of African

American women administrators in higher education. The data were analyzed for all subjects simultaneously. Finally, the findings of this research were reflected upon and discussed in chapter six in relation to theories and literature on black women in higher education, with particular emphasis on recruitment, retention, and promotion. Recommendations for further study on black women in higher education administration were also explored relative to this study.

Problems of Reliability and Validity

Exploratory research often generates questions about dependability of the investigative instrument to consistently accomplish what it was intended to accomplished.

Reliability and Validity

Reliability addresses a particular technique applied repeatedly (elaboration model) to the same factor, would yield the same result each time. It is concerned with how well the test used measures what it is suppose to measure (Babbie, 1990). Reliability is the extent to which a test measures what it is supposed to measure. Validity entails the extent to which an empirical measure sufficiently reflects the real meaning of the concept under consideration. Qualitative research generally results in high validity and low reliability. Babbie (1990) explains that field research seems to prove to be a valid measure of what is being studied. Qualitative research can provide a depth of meaning of concepts not found in other forms of research. Thus, it measures what it is supposed to measure providing a much greater level of understanding. Conversely, qualitative research suffers from low reliability in that the same account of an event will generally yield different interpretations of the environment (e.g., one researcher may interpret a behavior as appropriate and another may interpret the same behavior as inappropriate). The researcher must be aware of his/her tendency to bias data through both its observation and analysis.

In direct contrast to qualitative research, quantitative research (surveys) was used in this study. Surveys are generally considered to be weak on validity and strong reliability. Since the survey reduces issues and responses to the least common denominator, it puts a strain on validity. For example, the survey instrument may not have been constructed in such a way as to measure accurately an issue with regard to culture or context. Several limitations may have resulted that limited the validity of the data in regard to that specific context. Use of the Likert Response Scale in recording responses does not provide the freedom or validity that qualitative research does by recording responses more like a continuous variable than a discrete one.

In survey research, one can only assume the level of agreement or disagreement with the results that are ambiguous at best. On the other hand, standardizing the survey instrument used can provide strong reliability by eliminating the bias of the researcher. Data and information from survey instruments is empirical in nature and easily tested for reliability by other means. By careful, thorough construction of the survey instrument, respondents ambiguity can be reduced as well.

Therefore, the quantitative research surveys was selected as the best method to use for this exploratory, descriptive study. Further, the surveys allowed the researcher to survey a larger number of respondents to participate in the investigation of the recruitment, retention, and promotion patterns.

Summary

This chapter presented the choice of research instrument and rationale for that choice. It also presented and further clarified the terms used in the study, population and sampling procedures, survey implementation, format/design, survey pretest, data analyzes and data reporting.

Chapter IV

Presentation and Discussion of Subjects

This was an exploratory, descriptive study conducted to identify possible relationships between African American administrators' education and their recruitment, retention, and promotion opportunities. It focused on two essential questions and three guiding questions. The first essential question: What are the internal factors that may impact African American women administrators' recruitment, retention, and promotion patterns? The second essential question: What are the external factors that may impact African American women administrators' recruitment, retention, and promotion patterns? The three guiding questions that resulted from the two essential questions were: (1) Does the administrators' education (bachelor's, master's or doctorate degree) have an impact on employment opportunities (job offers)?, (2) Does the administrators' current employment institution have an impact on the number of years in current position and promotion in higher education and at current institution?, and (3) Does the institution from which the individual earned the professional degrees have an impact on current employment, current retention and promotion? The presentation and discussion of the profile of subjects will not include every question asked on the survey. The information obtained from some questions is in some cases counterfactual (e.g. CEO gender was reported to contradict a federal report of these statistics). Therefore three criteria were used to determine which questions were to be eliminated from the discussion: (1) if the researcher knew from the prior response rate the information was not correct (for example when asked to report CEO gender and ethnicity, respondents reported 58% male and 42% female—1993 statistics from the American Council on Education reported 88% white male and 12% white female); (2) if questions were not clear to respondents (for example, when asked if there is not only a "glass-ceiling" at my institution, but a "colored glass" ceiling—many respondents wrote the question was not clear and that they had not heard of the term "colored glass" ceiling;) and, (3) if responses were so diverse that the researcher had difficulty in collapsing the data (for example respondents were asked the size of the budgets they manage—the responses ranged from $37.60 to 6 million dollars).

Profile of Subjects

Before examining the two essential questions in detail, it is necessary first to present a picture of the respondents who participated in the study. Therefore, a description of the respondents who participated in the study are provided in this section. The profile includes information on respondents' (1) current professional position, (2) institution, (3) age, (4) marital status, (5) family, (6) experience in higher education, (7) experience in administration, (8) previous position, (9) promotion history, and (10) previous education. Table 1 depicts seven of these categories of background information on respondents.

Current Position

This section examines information on respondents' current positions and the institutions at which they hold these positions. Of the 154 respondents, 15 (13%) hold positions as presidents, 42 (28%) as vice-presidents, 37 (24%) as deans, and 53 (35%) as directors, coordinators and supervisors.

Institutions

These administrators are located in both public and private institutions: 88 (61%) of the African American female administrators surveyed in this study are in public institutions and 55 (39%) are in private institutions. In addition, these institutions are divided into urban and rural categories, with 88 (62%) of these administrators located in urban institutions and 55 (38%) located in rural institutions. The institutions included in the study may be further identified by geographic region: 46 (32%) of the institutions are located in the northeast; 65 (44%) of the institutions are located in the southeast; and 35 (24%) of the institutions are located in the west. Finally the institutions at which these administrators work are identified by their historical origin: 49 (34%) are historically black institutions (HBIs) and 96 (66%) are traditionally white institution (TWI). In summary, the majority of African American female administrators in this study were employed as vice-presidents or deans in public traditionally white institutions, located in urban areas in the southeast region of the United States.

Basic Demographics

Table 1 presents information on the administrators' age, marital status, and family status such as two-career couple and number of children. Of the 151 respondents who provided age information, 125 (82.8%) are 40 years of age or older, and 26 (17.2%) are under the age of 39. In terms of marital status reported, 64 (43%) are married, 40 (27%) are single, and 46 (31%) are divorced. When asked if they consider themselves members of a two-career couple, 67 (45%) indicated yes and 83 (55%) indicated no. In addition, 94 (63%) of respondents have children and 56 (37%) do not have children. In summary, administrators are typically 40 years of age or older, are married or divorced, and have children. Respondents are about evenly divided in considering themselves members of two-career couples (respondents answering this question may have been divorced or widowed, or single living with a partner, or living in an alternate life-style relationship).

Previous Experience and Promotion History

Respondents were asked information about their previous professional experience and background. When asked the number of years in higher education; 121(84%) of these administrators have more than 10 years in higher education, 23 (16%) of the administrators have 10 years or fewer. In contrast, in terms of number of years as administrators, 61(85.6%) of these administrators have 10 or more years experience in administration and 56 (13.4%) of the administrators have fewer than 10 years experience in administration. When asked to describe

Table 1
Background of Respondents

Question	Number	%
Current Position		
Chancellor	4	2
President	19	12
Vice-President	42	27
Dean	37	24
Other	53	43
No responses	3	2
Public/Private		
Public	88	57
Private	55	36
No responses	11	7
Urban/Rural		
Urban	91	58
Rural	36	35
No responses	11	8
Region of Country		
Northeast	46	30
Southwest	65	42
West	35	23
No responses	8	5
HBC/TWI		
HBCs	49	32
TWIs	96	62
No responses	9	6
Age		
29 and under	4	3
30 - 39	22	14
40 - 49	62	40
50 and over	63	41
No responses	3	2
Marital Status		
Single	40	26
Married	64	42
Divorced	46	30
No responses	4	3

their previous position, 74 (52%) of respondents reported that their previous position was in the rank of executive staff (chancellor, president, vice-president, dean, or provost), 17 (12%) in professional staff (assistant to president or dean, executive assistant, special assistant, or administrative advisor), 42 (30%) in general administration (advisor, coordinator, and director), and 9 (6%) in support staff (assistant coordinator, counselor, and other). Respondents further described their previous position in terms of field of specialty. In this category, 57 (41%) respondents describe their previous positions as academic (reporting to the vice-president of academic affairs), 46 (33%) as administrative (reporting to the vice president of administration, student affairs, or student services), and 37 (26%) as student service (admissions, financial aid, student records, and counseling). Respondents were also asked their promotion history. Of the 148 responding to this question, 112 (76%) stated that they have been promoted in the last 5 years, while 36 (24%) stated that they have not been promoted. When asked if they have been promoted at their current institution in the last five years; 68 (53%) of these administrators stated that they had been promoted at their current institution. Respondents were asked to list the title of their promotion rank, 63 (90%) were promoted as executive staff, 5 (7%) as professional staff and 2 (3%) as general administration.

Respondents who reported promotions were also asked if additional benefits accompanied the promotion. Sixty-one (86%) of these administrators stated that additional benefits did accompany the promotion while 10 (14%) stated that they received no additional benefits. Respondents who reported that additional benefits accompanied their promotions were asked to identify the benefits. Benefits were reported and ranked in the following order, with 46 (84%) of the administrators receiving salary increases, and 9 (16%) of the administrators receiving increased responsibility. In summary, respondents had more than ten years of experience in higher education and higher education administration. They have held previous positions as executive staff members in academics, with the majority in higher education and at their current institution within the last five years. The benefits they received with promotion included increased salary and responsibilities.

Previous Education

Respondents' previous education was examined in terms of their doctoral, masters, and undergraduate program and degree experiences.

In regards to doctoral work, 102 (76%) reported having a doctoral degree, 15 (10%) are currently working on a doctorate, and 35 (23%) reported not having a doctorate degree. Of the respondents with a doctorate, 80 (70%) majored in education. At the masters level, 145 (96%) reported having a masters degree, while 5 (4%) reported that they do not have a masters degree, and 1 (.6%) reported that they are working on degree currently. Of these, 91(62%) majored in education. At the undergraduate level, 154 (100%) reported having a bachelor's degree. Field of specialty for undergraduate degree was not requested from respondents.

In summary, administrators reported having a doctorate degree in education; and, a small number of administrators are currently working on a doctorate degree. Doctoral and masters degrees are in education with less than one percent of administrators' reporting that they were still working on a doctoral degree.

Administrators Tasks and Functions

The types of responsibilities which respondents reported are as tasks and functions of their current position. In terms of the number of individuals who the respondents supervise, 117 (80%) of them supervised five or more people.

Scholarly and Creative Activities

A great deal of respondents' time is spent in areas outside of their regular duties (e.g. community activities, volunteer programs, grant writing and dissertation research). In terms of research, 151(92%) engage in some form of research with 6 (4%) of these engaging in research on a frequent basis, 30 (20%) often engaging in research, 54 (36%) occasionally engage in research, 49 (32%) seldom engage in research and 12 (8%) never engage in research. Respondents were also asked to list four types scholarly activities (e.g., workshops, newsletters, conference papers, articles and books). Among these activities, 140 (92%) of respondents reported conducting workshops, 88 (59%) presenting conference papers; 71 (47%) publishing books or journal articles and 64 (42%) of administrators writing newsletters.

Professional Involvement

Outside of their research activities, respondents commented on their involvement in professional organizations, 100 (68%) of administrators are involved in local organizations, 122 (84%) in regional organizations and 138 (90%) in national organizations (This involvement could be membership or holding office in prominent professional organizations).

Professional Service

Respondents' were asked to report on their involvement in the local white community and black community, 107 (74%) are involved in the local white community and 88 (82%) in the local black community. When asked what types of community organization involvement they engage in, 59 (50%) of respondents reported they are involved in community issues through such institutions as NAACP, Urban League, and Church, 15 (13%) in educational issues through such organizations as PTAs, Black Achievers, and School Boards), 17 (14%) in minority affairs participating on Black Chamber of Commerce and Multicultural Committee boards, 19 (16%) in women/sorority issues through involvement in Battered Women Shelters and national African American sororities (Delta Sigma Theta, Alpha Kappa Alpha and Zeta Phi Beta Sorority), and 9 (8%) involved in youth activity issues through Boy Scout and Girl Scouts troops.

Administrative Attitudes

Respondents were asked to respond to items designed to reveal how they feel about their position and, current institution, including campus environment, specifically signs that blacks are welcome on campus, and indicators of racial an sexual discrimination in the workplace. First, respondents described their feelings about their institution. In this area, 117 (97%) reported feeling good to excellent about working at their institution, while 23 (15%) reported feeling fair and 12 (8%) reported feeling poor. Respondents were also asked about their feelings toward their responsibilities, if they feel their responsibilities are the same as other administrators. To this item, 75 (51%) of these administrators reported that they feel their responsibilities are the same as those of other administrators, and 73 (49%) of the administrators feel that their responsibilities are not the same as those of other administrators. When asked if they consider their administrative power to be the same as that of other administrators, 45 (30%) feel their administrative power is the same as other administrators, 95 (64%) feel their administrative power is not the same, and 9 (6%) of administrators were unsure.

Next, respondents were ask if their institution has helped to assist in their professional development. One hundred fifteen (78%) felt that their institutions has been helpful in promoting their professional development, 20 (14%) do not feel that their institutions has been helpful, with professional development, and 12 (8%) were unsure of their feeling concerning their professional development.

Next respondents were asked if they feel isolated from white staff at their institution. To this item, 21(15%) reported that they feel isolated from white staff, 108 (77%) reported that they do not feel isolated from white staff, and 11(8%) of these administrators were not sure. When asked if they feel isolated from black staff at their institution, 20 (14%) of these African American administrators reported that they feel isolated from black staff at their institution, 122 (83%) do not feel isolated from black staff, and 5 (3%) of were unsure. Next, respondents were asked if they belong to a support group for African American women administrators at their institution. Fifty-nine (39%) belong to support groups for African American faculty and staff, 77 (57%) do not belong to support groups, and 6 (4%) of these administrators were unsure. Further, the majority of administrators reported that they feel white males and females are intimidated by their presence. When respondents were asked if they feel white males are intimidated by their presence, 64 (43%) feel that white males are intimidated by their presence and 66 (45%) feel that white females are intimidated by their presence. When asked if they feel black males are intimidated by their presence, 26 (18%) reported that they feel black males are intimidated by their presence and 48 (32%) feel that other black females are intimidated by their presence.

Respondents were asked if there are advantages to being an African American female at their institution. To this item, 88 (61%) reported they feel there are advantages, 34 (23%) feel there are not any advantages, and 16% were unsure.

In addition, thirty-six (25%) of respondents reported that they feel institutions prefer married administrators, 56 (39%) reported that they do not feel institutions prefer married administrators, and 52 (36%) were unsure.

Then the final question in this section asked respondents if they feel that their institution has support from the local white community. One hundred-twenty two (81%) respondents reported they feel their institution has support from local white community. When asked if their institution has support from the local black community 95 (64%) reported that feel their institution has support from the local black community. Support from the local white and black community may impact respondents' campus environment. Respondents were asked to comment on the campus environment. When asked if the feel there are signs on their campus that indicate to them that blacks are not welcomed, 36 (25%) reported that they feel there are such signs on their campus, 87 (62%) reported that they do not feel such signs are present on their campus, and 18 (13%) were unsure. Then, when respondents were asked if they feel their presence helps the racial climate at their institution, 13 (79%) reported that they feel their presence helps the racial climate on their campus, 17 (12%) reported that they do not feel their presence helps the racial climate, and 13 (9%) were unsure.

If there are signs at the institutions that promote feelings that black are not welcomed, freedom to socialize with non-African American administrators after work may be affected (e.g.. such signs may have been put in place intentionally by non-African Americans). When respondents were asked if they feel that they socialize with non-African American administrators outside of work, 17 (12%) reported that they socialize on a frequent basis with non-African American administrators outside of work, 24 (16%) reported that they socialize non-African Americans often, 41 (28%) reported that they socialize with non-African Americans seldom, 54 (36%) reported they occasionally socialize with non-African Americans, and 12 (9%) reported that they never socialize with non-African American administrators outside of work.

Socializing or not socializing with non-African American administrators outside of work could be due to several factors. The next section of items were designed to produce information that might clarify socialization responses. When asked if they have experienced racial prejudice in higher education, 115 (78%) reported that they feel they have experienced racial prejudice, 22 (15%) reported that they do not feel they have experienced racial prejudice, and 11(7%) were not sure. When respondents were asked if race played a role in their leaving one institution to go to another institution, 32 (24%) reported that race did play a major role in their leaving their last institution, 98 (73%) reported that race did not play a major role in their leaving their last institution and 5 (4%) were unsure. When ask if race played a major role in their coming to their present institution, 72 (50%) reported that they felt race did play a major role in their coming to their present institution, 62 (43%) reported that they feel race did not play a role in their coming to their present institution, and 10 (7%) were unsure. When asked if they feel their appointment to their current position was a sign of "tokenism," 17 (12%) reported that they feel their appointment was "tokenism," 111(77%) reported that they do not feel their appointment was "tokenism," and 17 (12%) were unsure.

The last question in this section asked if respondents have experienced sexual discrimination at their institution. One hundred and eight (73%) administrators reported that they feel they have experienced sexual discrimination, 27 (18%) reported that they do not feel they have experienced racial discrimination, and 14 (9%) were unsure.

In summarizing, most administrators reported the following:

1) They feel good about where they work.
2) Their responsibilities are the same as other administrators on their campus.
3) Their administrative power is the same as that of other administrators on their campus.
4) Institutions support their professional development.
5) Their appointment is not perceived as "tokenism."
6) Isolation is not a factor in their experience.
7) White males and females feel intimidated by their presence.
8) There are advantages to being an African American female administrator on their campus.
9) Institutions of higher education prefer married administrators.
10) Administrators receive support from both the black and white communities.
11) There are not signs of these administrators' campuses that blacks are not welcome.
12) The presence of Administrator helps to improve racial climate their institution.
13) These administrators seldom socialize with non-African American administrators outside of work.
14) Racial and Sexual discrimination has been experienced by these administrators.

15) Race did not play a role in these administrators' leaving one institution to go to another.
16) Race did play a role in these administrators coming to their present institution.
17) Most administrators received promotions within the last five years at TWIs.
18) Their doctorate and masters degree were obtained at TWIs.

TWI/HBCs Characteristics

Several questions were related to respondents' affiliation with their current institutions (HBIs and TWIs.) This section will lead into the next section of data analysis that emphasizes TWI/HBI as one of the main variables used in the analysis.

Promotions

When asked if their promotion occurred at an HBI or TWI, within the last five years, 44 (36%) respondents reported that their promotions took place at HBC and 76 (66%) reported that their promotions took place at TWIs.

Previous Education

When asked where they received their doctorate degree, 102 (98%) respondents reported that they received their doctorate from TWIs and 2 (2%) reported they received their doctorate from HBIs. Eighty (70%) of doctoral degrees received were in the field of education. One hundred-twenty one (95%) of respondents reported that they received their masters degree from TWIs and 6 (5%) from HBIs. Ninety-one (62%) respondents received their masters in the field of education. Twenty-five (19%) of respondents reported that they received their undergraduate degree from HBIs and 110 (81%) from TWIs.

Summary

This section presented information on the profile of subjects, current professional position, institution, basic demographics, previous experience and promotional history, previous education, administrative tasks and functions; scholarly and creative activities, professional involvement, professional service, administrative attitudes, TWI/HBI characteristics, and promotions.

Chapter V

Statistical Data Analysis

In the previous chapter, a description of administrators located at historically black institutions (HBIs) and traditionally white institutions (TWIs) is given. This chapter will describe the HBI/TWI relationships through the use of the elaboration model.

Elaboration

Throughout the 1950's and 1960's, multivariate analysis with contingency tables usually involved a simple technique known as elaboration (Lazarsfeld 1955, 1993). The elaboration model, used to understand the relationship between two variables through the simultaneous introduction of additional variables, describes the statistical relationships. This method was selected for data analysis. This method differs from qualitative research in the way in which the data is analyzed. Elaboration involves collecting data from survey research techniques similar to qualitative research, but the investigator assumes some hypotheses from the beginning. Rather than simply reporting observation, the researcher, using this technique, will assess the impact of different variables on some measurable outcomes through the controlled introduction of other variables (Internal and external factors). Internal factors used in this study are those of which the administrator has personal control over their existence. External factors are those over which the institution has control.

Research Questions Analyzed

This research was designed to answer two essential questions using the elaboration model. What internal factors impact African American women administrators' recruitment, retention, and promotion patterns? What external factors impact African American women administrators' recruitment, retention, and promotion patterns?

Three guiding questions were used in the analysis: What is the relationship between where an administrator received her education, and the number of job offers she received after receiving her bachelor's and doctorate degrees? What is the relationship between an administrators' current employment institution and number of years in current position, number of promotions in higher education, and promotions at the current institution? What is the relationship between where an administrator received her education and her current employment institution, number of years in higher education, number of years in current position, promotions in higher education and promotions at the current institution?

Internal and External Factors used in Analysis

The following internal and external factors were used as control variables in the study:

Internal Factors
1. Years in current position
2. Report of having a mentor
3. Report of engaging in networking
4. Field of study
5. Report of socializing with non-African American administrators.
6. Report of belonging to a support group
7. Doctorate degree year
8. Undergraduate degree year

External Factors
1. Current position
2. Employment opportunities after doctorate degree

3. Employment opportunities after undergraduate degree
4. African American female administrators on campus
5. African American male administrators on campus Findings/ Results

Results for Guiding Question 1

Administrators' undergraduate institution (Q10) was cross-tabulated with number of employment opportunities after the undergraduate degree (Q82). There was no significant relationship between type of institution (HBI or TWI) and number of job offers (three or fewer versus more than three). Eight-three administrators reported they had employment opportunities after completion of undergraduate degree. Of this number, 40 (48%) had three or less employment opportunities, and 43 (52%) had greater than three opportunities. Non-significant relationships were also obtained when year of undergraduate degree (Q9) was used as a control variable. Of the 38 administrators that reported they had their undergraduate degree by 1969 or earlier, 18 (47%) had more than three opportunities. Forty-two administrators had received their undergraduate degree by 1970 or later. Twenty (48%) had three or less employment opportunities and 22 (52%) had greater than three opportunities. Administrators' undergraduate institution (Q10) was cross-tabulated with the number of employment opportunities after the doctoral degree (Q83). There was no significant relationship between type of institution (HBI or TWI) and number of job offers (three or fewer versus more than three). Fifty-eight administrators reported having employment opportunities after obtaining their doctorate degrees. Of this number, 26 (45%) had less than three employment opportunities, and 32 (55%) had greater than three employment opportunities.

Non-significant relationships were also obtained when the doctoral degree field of study (Q16) was used as a control variable. Education was reported as the field of study for 38 administrators. Of this number, 17 (45%) had three or less employment opportunities, and 21 (55%) had greater than three employment opportunities. Nineteen administrators reported that education was not their field of study. Nine (47%) of these administrators had three or less employment opportunities and 10 (53%) had greater than three.

Summary of Data Analysis for Guiding Question 1

There was no significant relationship between type of education institution and number of job offers after the undergraduate degree. Data was not affected by the year in which the degree was obtained. There was no significant relationship between type of undergraduate institution and not affected by the field of study of the degree.

Results for Guiding Question 2

The administrators' current institution (Q1) was cross-tabulated with years in current position Q3). No significant relationship was observed for the 143 respondents that reported; 67 (47%) of administrators had been in their current position two years or less while 76 (53%) reported being in their current position greater than two years.

The following non-significant relationships were observed for the elaboration of Q1 and Q3 controlling for several of the previously listed internal and external factors.

Report of currently having a mentor (Q93)

Out of a total of 74 respondents who reported currently having a mentor, 36 (49%) have been in their current position two years or less and 38 (51%) had been in their current position longer than two years. Out of the 65 respondents reporting not having a position and 36 (55%) had greater than two years.

Report of engaging in networking (Q92)

Sixty-eight (50%) administrators responded they engaged in networking; 39 (57%) of these administrators had been in their current position two years or less, and 29 (43%) had been in their current position longer than two years. The other sixty-eight administrators reported no engagement in networking; 26 (38%) administrators had two years or less in their current position and 42 (62%) of administrators had greater than two years.

Statistical Data Anaylsis 63

Report of socializing with non-African American administrators (Q46)

Of the 37 administrators who reported they frequently socialized with non-African American administrators, 19 (51%) had two years or less in their current position, and 18 (49%) had more than two years. Out of 50 respondents who reported they occasionally socialized with non- African American administrators, 23 (46%) were in their current position two years or less while 27 (54%) had greater than two years. Forty-nine respondents reported they seldom socialized with non-African American administrators. Of these women, 21 (43%) had two years or less in their current position and 28 (57%) had more than two years in their current position.

Report of belonging to a support group (Q75)

Seventy-five administrators reported they do not belong to a support group. Of this number, 37 (49%) had been in their current position two years or less, and 38 (51%) had been in their current position greater than two years. A smaller number of administrators (44) reported they do belong to a support group with 17 (39%) having been in their current position two years or less and 27 (61%) in their current position greater than two years.

Current position title (Q2)

Eighteen administrators reported their current position as president. Of this number, 13 (72%) had been in their present position two years or less, and 5 (29%) had been in their position longer than two years. Of the 41 vice presidents, 19 (46%) had two years or less in their current position, and 22 (54%) had more than two years. Thirty-five administrators reported their current position as dean with 17 (49%) of this number having been in their current position less than two years and 18 (51%) having more than two years in their present position. Of the 49 administrators in positions classified as "other" (directors, coordinators, and supervisors), 18 (37%) had two years or less in their current position and 31 (63%) had more than two years.

Doctorate degree year (Q14)

Forty-five administrators reported not having a doctorate degree with 21 (47%) that reported they had been in their current position two years or less and 24 (53%) having greater than two years. Of the 96 administrators that reported they do have a doctorate degree, 45 (47%) had been in their current position two years or less, and 51 (53%) had greater than two years in current position.

Administrators' employment institution (Q1) and number of years in higher education (Q6) were cross-tabulated, and a non-significant relationship was found. The following were used as control variables: report of currently having a mentor, report of belonging to a support group, engaging in networking, and socializing with non-African American administrators. No significant effects were found.

Report of currently having a mentor (Q93)

A substantial number (71) of administrators reported they currently have a mentor. Of this number, 30 (42%) have been in higher education 15 years or less, and 41 (58%) have more than 15 years in higher education. Sixty-four administrators reported they do not have a mentor with 15 (23%) having 15 years or less and 49 (77%) having more than 15 years.

Report of belonging to a support group (Q75)

Of the 72 administrators reporting they do not currently belong to a support group, 24 (33%) have 15 years or less in higher education, and 48 (67%) have more than 15 years. Forty-four administrators reported they belong to a support group with 20 (45%) having 15 years or less in higher education and 24 (54%) having more than 15 years.

Report of engaging in networking (Q92)

Networking was reported to be engaged in by 63 administrators. Of this number, 22 (35%) had 15 years or less and 41 (65%) had greater than 15 years. Sixty-eight administrators reported they did not engage in networking with 23 (34%) having 15 years or less in higher education and 45 (66%) having more than 15 years.

Socialization with non-African American administrators (Q46)

A small number of administrators (33) reported they socialized on a frequent basis with non-African American administrators. Of this number 8 (24%) had 15 years or less, and 25 (76%) had more than 15 years. Fifty-one administrators reported they occasionally socialize with non-African American administrators with 16 (31%) had 15 years or less and 35 (69%) had more than 15 years. Of the 49 administrators that reported they seldom socialized with non- African American administrators, 21 (43%) had 15 years or less, and 28 (57%) had more than 15 years.

Report of currently having a mentor (Q93)

A number of administrators (71) reported they currently had a mentor. Of this number, 56 (79%) had been promoted in higher education within the last five years, and 15 (21%) had not been promoted. Sixty-four administrators reported they do not currently have a mentor with 47 (73%) reporting they had been promoted within higher education and 17 (27%) having not been promoted.

Report of belonging to a support group (75)

Of the 74 administrators that reported they do not belong to a support group, 56 (76%) have been promoted within higher education during the last five years and 18 (24%) had not been promoted. Forty- three administrators reported they belong to a support group with 31 (72%) having been promoted within higher education and 12 (28%) had not been promoted.

Engaging in networking (Q92)

Several administrators (66) reported engagement in networking with 52 (79%) being promoted within the last five years while 14 (21%) had not. Sixty-five administrators reported that they do not engage in networking with 50 (77%) who had been promoted within higher education and 15 (23%) who had not been promoted.

Socialization with non-African American administrators (Q46)

Thirty-five administrators reported they socialized with non- African American administrators on a frequent basis. Of the number, 29 (83%) reported they had been promoted within the last five years in higher education, and 6 (17%) had not been promoted. Of the 49 administrators that reported they occasionally socialized with non-African American administrators, 35 (71%) reported they had been promoted, and 14 (29%) had not been promoted. Forty-eight administrators reported they seldom socialized with non-African American administrators with 36 (75%) reporting they had been promoted in higher education and 12 (25%) who had not been promoted.

Administrators' promotions at their current institutions within the last five years (Q88) was cross-tabulated with administrators' employment institutions (Q1). A significant relationship was found (chi-square=6.93, df=1, p<01). For the 43 persons employed at HBIs, 70% reported getting a promotion in the last five years. However, only 45% of the 74 persons employed at a TWI were promoted. A number of significant and non-significant relationships resulted from the use of control variables.

Report of currently having a mentor (Q93)

A substantial number of administrators (60) reported they currently have a mentor with 37 (62%) having been promoted within the last five years at their current institution and 23 (38%) not having been promoted. Of the 57 administrators that reported they do not currently have a mentor, 79% of persons employed at HBIs reported getting a promotion in the last five years in contrast to 29% of employees of TWIs. This was statistically significant (chi-square=12.76, df, $p < .001$).

Report of belonging to a support group (Q75)

A significant relationship was observed for 64 administrators that reported they do not belong to a support group. For these persons, 70% of individuals employed at HBIs reported getting a promotion, but only 44% of persons employed at a TWI. This was statistically significant (chi-square=4.34, 1 df, $p < .04$). Thirty-eight administrators reported they do belong to a support group with 22 (58%) having been promoted at their current institution within the last five years and 16 (42%) having not been promoted.

Engaging in networking (Q92)

Of the 54 administrators that reported they engage in networking, 28 (52%) have been promoted at their current institution, and 26 (48%) had not been promoted. A significant relationship was observed] for 59 administrators who reported no involvement in networking. For those persons, 77% who worked at HBIs reported promotions, but only 39% of those who worked at TWIs. This was statistically significant (chi-square=8.87, 1 df, $p < .003$).

Socialization with non-African American administrators (Q46)

A number of administrators (30) reported they frequently socialized with non-African American administrators with 11 (37%) having been promoted at their current institution and 19 (63%) having not been promoted. Forty-two administrators reported they occasionally socialized with non-African American administrators. Of this number, 24 (57%) had been promoted at their current institution, and 18 (43%) had not been promoted. A significant relationship was observed for 41 administrators that reported they seldom socialized with non-African American administrators. For this group, 85% who worked at HBIs received a promotion, but only 38% of those at TWIs were promoted. This was statistically significant (chi-square=9.47, 1 df, $p < .003$).

Summary of Data Analysis for Guiding Question 2

There was no significant relationship between type of employment institution and number of years in current position. Data was not affected by having a mentor, engaging in networking, socializing with non-African American administrators, belonging to a support group, current position title, or having a doctoral degree.

There was significant relationship between type of employment institution and number of years in higher education. Data was not affected by having a mentor, belonging to a support group, engaging in networking, or socializing with non-African American administrators.

There was no significant relationship between type of employment institution and promotion within the last five years. Data was not affected by having a mentor, belonging to a support group, engaging in networking, or socializing with non-African American administrators.

There were significant relationships (p < .05) between type of employment institution and promotion in last five years at the current institution. A larger percentage of persons employed at HBIs got promoted than those employed at TWIs for the following reasons: administrators not having a mentor, not belonging to a support group, not engaging in networking, and seldom socializing with non-African-American administrators.

Results for Guiding Question 3

Administrators' undergraduate institution (Q10) was cross-tabulated with their employment institution (Q1) for the result of several significant relationships.

There was a significant association between education institution and employment institution (chi-square=8.85, df=1, p < .0030). Of the 21 persons who attended a HBI, 62% were employed by an HBI. However, of the 87 persons who attended as HBI, only 28% were employed by an HBI. The effects of several control variables were studied.

Socialization with non-African American administrators (Q46)

A significant relationship was observed for 35 administrators that reported they frequently socialized with non-African American administrators. For those persons, 75% of those educated at HBI's were employed by HBI's, but only 10% of those educated at TWI's were employed by HBI's (chi-square=10.64, df=1, p < .002). Forty-six administrators reported they occasionally socialized with non-African American administrators with 17 (37%) form HBIs and 29 (63%) from TWIs.

Another significant relationship was observed for 40 administrators that seldom socialized with non-African American administrators. For those persons, 80% of those educated at HBI's were employed by HBI's, but only 40% of those educated at TWI's were employed by HBI's (chi-square=4.8, df=1 p < .03).

Report of belonging to a support group (Q75). 1

A significant relationship was observed for 67 administrators that reported they do not belong to a support group. For those persons, 73% of those educated at HBI's were employed at HBI's, but only 39% of those educated at TWI's were employed by HBI's (chi-square=5.69, df=1, p < .02).

A significant relationship also was observed for 40 administrators that reported they belong to a support group. For these, 60%, of those educated at HBI's were employed by HBI's, but only 11% of those educated at TWI's were employed by HBI's (chi- square=7.15, df=1, p < .01).

Engage in networking (Q92)

Sixty-one administrators reported they engaged in networking. Of those, 63% who went to HBI's were employed by HBI's, but only 19% of those who attended TWI's worked at HBI's, (chi-square=7.13, df=1, p < .01). Sixty people reported not engaging in networking. Of those, 85% who went to HBI's were employed by HBI's, but only 40 of those who attended TWI's worked at HBI's (chi-square=7.95, df=1, p < .005).

Report of currently having a mentor (Q93)

Sixty-seven administrators reported they had a mentor. Of those, 80% who went to HBI's were employed by HBI's, but only 29% of those who went to TWI's worked at HBI's (chi-square-12.66, df=1, p < .001). Fifty-seven administrators reported that they do not currently have a mentor. Of this number, 18 (32%) were educated at HBI's and 39 (68%) at TWI's.

Administrators' undergraduate institution (Q10) was cross-tabulated with years in current position (Q3) for a number of non- significant relationships.

Socialization with non-African American administrators (Q46)

A number of administrators (36) reported they frequently socialized with non-African American administrators. Of the 36 administrators, 18 (50%) had two years or less in their current position, and 18 (50%)

had greater than two years. Forty-five administrators reported they occasionally socialized with non- African American administrators with 21 (47%) having two years or less and 24 (53%) more than two years. Of the 43 administrators who reported seldom socializing with non-African American administrators, 18 (42%) had two years or less and 25 (58%) had greater than two years.

Report of belonging to a support group (Q75)

Of the 68 administrators that reported they do not belong to a support group, 34 (50%) had two years or less in their current position, and 34 (50%) had greater than two years. Forty-two administrators reported they belonged to a support group with 14 (33%) having two years or less in their current position and 28 (68%) having greater than two years.

Engaged in networking (Q92)

Several administrators (62) reported they engaged in networking. Of this number, 36 (58%) had two years or less in their current position, and 26 (42%) had greater than two years. Sixty-three administrators reported they do not engage in networking with 23 (36%) having two years or less in their current position and 40 (63%) having greater than two years.

Report of currently having a mentor (Q93)

Seventy administrators reported they currently have a mentor. Of this number, 32 (46%) had been in their current position two years or less, and 38 (46%) had been in their current position two years or less, and 38 (54%) had greater than two years. Of the 57 administrators that reported they do not currently have a mentor, 27 (47%) had two years or less in their current position, and 30 (53%) had more than two years.

Number of years worked in higher education (Q6) was cross-tabulated with administrators' undergraduate degree institution (Q10) for one significant relationship and a number of non- significant relationships with the following variables.

Report of belonging to a support group (Q75)

Several administrators (66) reported no support group affiliation with 24 (36%) having 15 years or less in higher education and 42 (64%) more than 15 years. Forty-two administrators reported current support group affiliation. Of this number, 15 (36%) had 15 years or less in higher education, and 27 (64%) had greater than 15 years.

Report of engaging in networking (Q92)

A significant relationship was observed for 59 administrators engaging in networking. For those educated at ant HBI, 3.3% were employed more than 15 years. For those educated at a TWI, 72% were employed more than 15 years. This was statistically significant (chi-square, df=1, p < .03). Sixty-three administrators reported they do not engage in networking with 21 (33%) having less than 15 years in higher education and 42 (67%) having more than 15 years.

Socialization with non-African American administrators (Q46)

A small number of administrators (33) reported they socialized with non-African American administrators on a frequent basis. Of this number, 8 (24%) had 15 years or less in higher education, and 25 (76%) had more than 15 years. Forty-six administrators reported they occasionally socialized with non-African American administrators with 15 (33%) having 15 years or less in higher education and 31 (67%) having greater than 15 years. Of the 44 administrators that reported they seldom socialized with non- African American administrators, 18 (41%) had 15 years or less in higher education, and 26 (59%) had more than 15 years.

Report of currently having a mentor (Q93)

A number of administrators (69) reported they currently have a mentor. Of this number, 27 (39%) had 15 years or less in higher education, and 42 (61%) had greater than 15 years. Fifty-six administrators reported they do not have a mentor with 14 (25%) having

15 years or less in higher education and 42 (75%) having more than 15 years.

Promotions within the last five years in higher education (Q85) was cross-tabulated with administrators' undergraduate degree institution (Q10) with a number of control variables.

Socialization with non-African American administrators (Q46)

A significant relationship was observed for a small number of administrators (34) that reported frequent socialized with non- African American administrators. For this group, 50% (2 of 4) of the people educated at an HBI were promoted in the last five years, but 93% (28 of 30) persons educated at a TWI were promoted (chi-square=6.38, df=1, p < .02). Forty-four administrators reported they occasionally socialized with non-African American females with 31 (71%) reporting they had been promoted within higher education the last five years and 13 (29%) not having a promotion within those five years. Of the 45 administrators that reported they seldom socialized with non-African American administrators, 32 (71%) had been promoted within higher education within the last five years, and 13 (29%) had not been promoted.

Report of belonging to a support group (Q75)

Sixty-eight administrators reported they do not belong to a support group. Of this number, 53 (78%) had been promoted in higher education within the last five years, and 15 (22%) had not been promoted. A smaller number of administrators (42) report support group affiliation with 28 (68%) having been promoted within the last five years and 14 (33%) not having been promoted.

Report of engaging in networking (Q92)

A total of 61 administrators (61) reported engagement in networking. Of this number, 48 (79%) had been promoted within higher education the last five years, and 13 (21%) had not been promoted. Of the 62 administrators that reported they do not engage in networking, 47 (76%) had been promoted within higher education the last five years, and 15 (24%) had not been promoted.

Report of currently having a mentor (Q93)

Seventy administrators reported they currently have a mentor with 55 (79%) having been promoted within higher education the last five years and 15 (21%) not having been promoted. Fifty-six administrators reported they do not currently have a mentor. Of this number, 41 (73%) have been promoted within higher education, and 15 (27%) have not been promoted.

Administrators' undergraduate institution (Q1) was cross-tabulated with promotions within the last five years at their current institution (Q88) for a number of non-significant relationships.

Socialization with non-African American administrators (Q46)

A few administrators (29) reported they frequently socialized with non-African American administrators. Of this number, 12 (41%) had been promoted at their current institution, and 17 (59%) had not been promoted. Thirty-eight administrators reported they occasionally socialized with non-African American administrators with 21 (55%) reporting they had received a promotion at their current institution within the last five years and 17 (45%) not being promoted at their current institution. Of the 40 administrators that reported they seldom socialized with non- African American administrators, 24 (60%) had been promoted at their current institution within the last five years, and 16 (40%) had not been promoted.

Report of belonging to a support group (Q75)

A non-significant relationship was observed for 59 administrators that reported they do not belong to a support group. Of this number 35 (59%) had been promoted at their current institution within the last five years, and 24 (41%) had been promoted. Thirty-eight administrators reported that they belonged to a support group, with 20 (53%) reporting they had been promoted and 18 (47%) not having been promoted.

Engaging in networking (Q92)

Of the 50 administrators that reported they engage in networking, 26 (52%) had been promoted at their current institution within the last five years, and 24 (48%) had not been promoted. Fifty-eight administrators reported they do not engage in networking with 34 (59%) reporting they had been promoted within their current institution and 24 (41%) had not been promoted.

Report of currently having mentor (Q93)

Sixty-one administrators reported they currently have a mentor. Of this number, 38 (62%) had been promoted at their current institution, and 23 (38%) had not been promoted. A smaller number of administrators (50) reported they do not currently have mentor with 22 (44%) reporting they have been promoted at their current institution and 28 (56%) not having been promoted.

Summary of Data Analysis for Guiding Question 3

When administrators' undergraduate institution was cross-tabulated with employment institution, several significant relationships were observed. Those educated at HBI's were more likely to be employed at HBI's, and those educated at TWI's were more likely to be employed at TWI's. This was true for those who socialized frequently or socialized seldom with non-African American administrators. A similar relationship between education and employment was found for those who did belong to a support group and those who did not, those who networked and those who did not, and those reported having a mentor.

The relationship between undergraduate institution and number of years in current position was not affected by socialization with non-African American administrators, belonging to a support group engaging in networking or having a mentor.

Undergraduate degree institution was cross-tabulated with number of years in higher education. For those who networked, a higher percentage of those educated at an TWI were employed for more than 15 years than were those educated at an HBI. Belonging to a support group, socialization with non-African American administrators and having a mentor were not significant control variables.

Cross-tabulating undergraduate institution with promotions in higher education led to one significant relationship. For those who frequently socialized with non-African American administrators, a higher percentage of those educated at a TWI were promoted than those educated at an HBI. The control variable of support group, networking, and having a mentor were not significant.

Finally, undergraduate institution was cross-tabulated with promotions obtained at the current institution. No significant effects were obtained when examining the control variables for socialization with non-African American administrators, belonging to a support group engaging in networking and having a mentor.

Chapter VI

Discussion and Recommendations

This study was conducted in an effort to explore and describe patterns of recruitment, retention, and promotion of African American women administrators in higher education. A discussion will follow on the impact of internal and external factors framed within the "human capital theory" approach.

A number of relationships were observed based upon the three guiding questions: (1) What is the relationship between where an administrator obtained her education and the number of job offers after completion of a bachelor's and doctorate degrees? (2) What is the relationship between the administrator's current employment institution and opportunities for retention and promotion? (3) What is the relationship between the administrators undergraduate institution and current employment institution, retention and promotion opportunities? Also, recommendations for additional research will be presented.

African American women administrators are few in number but vital to the endeavors of higher education. The fact that so few of these women are found in both HBIs and TWIs makes this research important. The information obtained in the study contributes to the completion of an overall picture of black women in higher education administration. Based on information from this exploratory and descriptive study, a number of recommendations can be made for recruiting, retaining, and promoting this group of women into administrative positions.

Discussion of Subjects

A composite of characteristics of African American women administrators emerged from the data. The results of this composite were surprising to the researcher based upon her prior assumptions about these women. Basic demographic information on African American women in higher education presented by Johnson (1991) in her research on factors affecting workplace performance was confirmed in this study. The majority of administrators reported they were an average of 40 years of age or older and married with children. Harvard (1986) discovered these women reportedly are located in urban institutions. They consider themselves to be a part of a "two-career" couple.

Respondents were asked to report on previous education and background experience. As Moses (1989) previously proposed, these women had more than ten years in experience in higher education, as a higher education administrator. Their previous positions held consisted basically of executive staff positions in academics which is basically where African American women begin their careers in higher education. Gill and Showell (1986) reported on the Cinderella concept of the black female in higher education, and their successful progression. The majority of administrators reported they had been promoted at their current institution and in higher education within the last five years. Basically, the promotions consisted of increased responsibilities and salary.

Howard-Vital (1987) depicted in their study that African American females should pursue the doctoral degree to advance their careers, and apparently, African American women have heeded the recommendation. In this study, the majority of the respondents had their doctorate degree primarily in the field of education. A small number of administrators were presently working on their doctorate degree.

Jones (1991) stated that African American women felt good about their work and responsibilities. Administrators were asked to respond to several questions involving expressing their feelings about their current position and work environment. Respondents stated they felt good about where they work. They felt that their responsibilities were basically, the same as non- African American administrators. However, they did not feel their administrative power was the same. Alexander and Scott (1983) had commented on the fact that African American women in academe must basically, make their presence known and felt. Several issues were raised by African American women administrators in the focus group about the following areas of concern:

Discussion and Recommendations

1. Institutions were supportive of their professional development.
2. Administrative power was the same as other administrators on campus.
3. Administrative appointment was not viewed as tokenism.
4. Feelings of isolation was not present with black and white staff members.
5. White males and females were perceived to be intimidated by their presence.
6. Advantages do exist for African American females on their campus.
7. The local black and white communities surrounding their campuses support administrators.
8. Signs (seen and unseen) that give the impression that blacks are not welcomed are not present on their campuses.
9. Administrators' presence helps to improve racial climate on campus.
10. Socialization with non-African American administrators is engaged on an occasional to seldom basis.
11. Racial and sexual discrimination was experienced by administrators in higher education.
12. Race played a role in administrators leaving one institution to go to another.
13. Race did not play a role in a administrator coming to their current institution.
14. Promotions were received in higher education and at their current institution within the last five years.
15. Masters and doctorate degrees were obtained from TWIs.

A discussion was presented on subjects' responses to their current position, institution, age, marital status, family experience in higher education and administration, previous position, promotion history, and previous education.

A primary focus of this study was to investigate the similarities between TWIs and HBIs administrators. A discussion of these similarities and differences was presented. Most administrators reported their promotions took place at an TWI. Information provided in Chapter II confirms the fact that HBIs have a small number of African American women administrators. Administrators commented in the focus group that African American women do not receive the recognition they deserve at HBIs.

Doctoral degrees were reportedly received most often from TWIs versus HBIs. This finding is not unusual since there are only five HBIs that are doctorate degree granting institutions. Mazon and Ross (1990) found that most African Americans received their graduate degrees in education. This researcher found the same to be true for the administrators participating in this study.

Of the 121 respondents that reported they had received their master's degrees, 91 received their degree in the field of education, and the degrees again were obtained from TWIs. A number of HBIs are certified to grant the master's of education degree. However, administrators in this study apparently preferred obtaining this degree from a TWI. The researcher might speculate that this phenomenon could be due to geographical location, family, or support issues.

Summary

African American women administrators who participated in this study appear typical of the general population. Although a small number of HBI administrators participated in the study, information provided by these administrators on their institutions, current positions and family was comprehensive in nature. A larger number of TWI administrators participated in the study and reported some interesting information on their institution, current position and family environment.

Discussion of Statistical Data Analysis

A discussion of the profile of respondents was presented in the previous section. This section will focus on the discussion about the data analysis. Darity (1982) identified accumulated earned income by blacks and whites as "human capital." Human capital is defined as any acquired skills, experience, or education an individual obtains which makes them more marketable. Human capital theory is an approach which this researcher borrowed from the field of human resource management and labor relations to frame this study.

The two essential research questions and three guiding questions are used to frame the data analysis. The internal and external factors are used as control variables throughout the data analysis enhancing the result of the three guiding questions.

Discussion and Recommendations 81

A discussion of the three guiding questions is presented with the results of the statistical tests of cross-tabulation:

1. *What is the relationship between where an administrator received her education and the number of job offers she received after completing her bachelor's and doctorate degrees?* Gill and Showell (1991) found in their study on the black female in higher education that job opportunities was not related to education but to "who you know." Undergraduate degree (Q10) was cross-tabulated with employment opportunities after doctorate (Q83) for a non- significant relationship. The majority of administrators 32 (55%) reported they had three or more employment opportunities after completion of their doctorate degree. Forty-three administrators (52%) reported they had three or more employment opportunities after completion of their undergraduate degree.

2. *What is the relationship between an administrators current employment institution and the number of years in current position, number of promotions in higher education within the last five years and number of promotions at current institution?* Johnson (1991) discovered in her study on factors affecting workplace performance that the majority of African American women administrators spend 1 - 5 years in their current position. Gill and Showell (1991) concluded in their research that African American women administrators had the same job title for the past four years.

Administrators' current institution (Q1) was cross-tabulated with years in current position (Q3) for a non-significant relationship. Most administrators 76 (53%) reported being in their current position greater than two years. Promotions within the last five years in higher education (Q88) was also cross-tabulated with (Q1) for a significant relationship. One hundred and nineteen administrators reported being promoted within higher education. Of this number, 45 (38%) were from HBIs and 74 (62%) were from TWIs.

Promotions at current institution (Q85) was cross-tabulated with (Q1) for two significant relationships. Out of a total of 112 administrators that reported they had been promoted , 41 (37%) had been promoted at an HBI, and 71 (63%) had been promoted at a TWI. One hundred and seven administrators reported they had been promoted. Of this number, 71 (66%) had been promoted at a TWI, and 36 (34%) had not been promoted.

3. *What is the relationship between where an administrator received her education (Q10) and her current employment institution (Q1), number of years in higher education (Q6), number of years in current position (Q3), promotions in higher education (Q85), and promotions at current*

institution (Q88)? Administrators' undergraduate institution (Q10) was cross- tabulated with their employment institution (Q1) for a significant relationship. One hundred and twenty administrators reported they have obtained their undergraduate degree. Of this number, 23 (18%) received their degree from an HBI, and 105 (82%) received their degree from an TWI.

The number of years worked in higher education (Q6) was cross-tabulated with (Q1) for a non-significant relationship. Of the 138 administrators that reported, 92 (67%) reported they had more than 15 years in higher education, and 46 (23%) had less than 15 years in higher education. The number of years worked in current position (Q3) was cross-tabulated with (Q1) for a non- significant relationship. One hundred and forty-one administrators reported with 66 (47%) had been in their current position more than two years. Promotions within higher education (Q85) and promotion within the current institution (Q88) was cross-tabulated with (Q1) for a significant relationship between (Q88) and (Q1) and a non- significant relationship between (Q85) and (Q1). One hundred and nineteen administrators reported on promotions at their current institution within the last five years. Of this number, 63 (53%) had been promoted, and 56 (47%) had not been promoted. Sixty-six administrators reported on promotions within higher education the last five years. Fifty-nine (89%) had been promoted and 5 (8%) had not been promoted.

Summary

The guiding questions for the study helped to frame the data analysis so that the external and internal factors could be introduced in the next section as control variables. A number of significant and non-significant relationships were observed for the analysis of these three questions. Some of the results correlated closely with previous research findings while some diverged from earlier findings.

Internal and External Factors Introduced as Control Variables.

The control variables were introduced into the three guiding questions through the procedure of the elaboration model (used to enhance the initial relationship between two variables). A discussion is provided on the impact of the internal and external factors on the three guiding questions.

1. Administrators' current institution (Q1) and years in current position (Q3) was cross-tabulated and the following results were obtained: Although administrators reported they had been in their current position more than two years, they do not engage in networking nor do they belong to a support group for African American faculty and staff. These administrators do however report having a mentor which is crucial to professional development. This may be due to what the Moynihan-Elkins School refers to as black families not socializing their youth to engage in such activities. The administrators in the study had completed their doctorate degrees which Moses (1989) stated was crucial for African American women in higher education. They also majored in education which is typical of African Americans.

Three or more employment opportunities were reported by administrators as available after completion of their undergraduate and doctoral degrees. Could it be that higher education is finally making progress in recognizing the deficiency of African Americans in higher education? Along with this same information, administrators reported that their are other African American male and female administrators on their campus.

2. Current employment institution (Q1) was cross-tabulated years in higher education (Q6) for a non-significant relationship with the following control variables: Again, administrators having a number of years of experience in higher education. A situation that is typical for African American women. They also reported having a mentor, not belonging to a support group or engaging in networking, and they occasionally to seldom socialized with non-African American administrators. In retrospect, this researcher would conclude that African American women administrators are seasoned professionals that are independent minded and self-motivated.

3. Administrators' employment institution (Q1) was cross-tabulated with promotions within higher education the last five years (Q88) for several non-relationships. The fact that administrators had been promoted within higher education the last five years did not have an effect on the initial control variables. Administrators continue to report that they did not engage in networking, belong to a support group, occasionally to seldom socialized with non-African American administrators and currently have a mentor.

4. Current employment institution (Q1) was cross-tabulated with undergraduate institution (Q10) for a number of significant relationships among the control variables: Administrators receiving their undergraduate degree from a HBI and TWI were primarily employed at TWIs. Are TWIs doing a better job than HBIs at recruiting African American women administrators? The majority of TWI administrators reported that they seldom socialized with non-African American administrators, do not belong to a support group, are evenly distributed on networking and non-networking, and currently have a mentor.

5. The number of years in current position (Q3) was cross-tabulated with the administrators' undergraduate institution (Q10) which resulted in non-significant relationships. Administrators receiving their undergraduate from both HBIs and TWIs reported they had two or more years in their current position. Again these women have not been in their current positions very long. Which may reflect again on higher education efforts to increase the number of African American women administrators. They also reported that they occasionally socialized with non-African American administrators, do not engage in networking or belong to a support group, but again currently have a mentor.

6. The number of years within higher education (Q6) was cross-tabulated with administrators' undergraduate institution (Q10) for the several non-significant relationships: Administrators from both HBIs and TWIs had approximately 15 years or more in higher education with the same results for the control variables listed earlier.

7. Promotions within the higher education the last five years (Q85) and administrators' undergraduate institution (Q10) again for a number of non-significant relationships among with the control variables. Most administrators (TWI and HBI) reported they had been promoted within higher education. The same administrators reported having a mentor, not engaging in networking or belonging to a support group, and occasionally socialized with non-African American administrators.

Discussion and Recommendations 85

8. Promotions at current institution (Q88) and (Q1) was cross tabulated for several non-significant relationships between administrators at HBIs and TWIs. Also reported the same results for the control variables.

Summary

The internal and external factors were cross-tabulated with the three guiding questions to produce a significant relationship between Administrators' employment institution (Q1) and undergraduate degree institution (Q10). All other remaining relationships were non-significant.

Concluding Comments.

This study confirmed some of my initial assumptions and expectations about African American women in higher education administration. They are listed as follows: employment opportunities, years in current position and in higher education, location of administrators (TWI or HBI), career advancement, and the level of education. The results of what this researcher discovered about her prior assumptions and expectations are provided below:

1. *Employment Institution (Q1).* The majority of African American women administrators, participating in this study, were employed at TWIs.
2. *Locating administrators to participate in the study.* Letters and telephone calls were received from TWIs volunteering information on the number of African American women administrators on their campuses.
3. *Lack of available information on career development, successful leadership opportunities, and strategies.* Administrators not only responded to the survey questions on these topics, but provided additional comments on the survey and in letters attached to the survey.
4. *Concentration of administrators in lower administrative ranks.* The majority of respondents held positions of director, coordinator and special assistant.

5. *Few African American women a administrative level at HBIs.* The number of administrators responding from HBIs was small. However, when administrators were asked about other African American female administrators on their campus, HBIs reported numbers were not any less than TWIs.
6. *Education related to advancement.* Administrators' reported that having a doctorate degree had a small impact upon their promotion opportunities.

Summary

Research conducted by earlier researchers in some instances did not show up in this study. For example, Tobin (1900) stated that most African American women administrators were located at HBIs. This researcher was surprised by some of the results because the situation in a lot of cases has not changed for African American women in higher education.

Recommendations

The research on African American women in higher education as discussed in Chapter II, and including this study of the recruitment, retention, and promotion patterns of these women, suggests African American women are making progress in the ranks of higher education, but more could be done on the part of institutions to eliminate racial and sexual barrier.

A number of recommendations for additional research resulting from this study include conducting further investigations on:

1. Type of College where administrators are located (junior college, college, or university).
2. Chief Executive Officer gender and ethnicity.
3. Geographical location of institutions where administrators are located.
4. Geographical location of doctorate granting degree institution.
5. Partner's effect on career mobility.

Discussion and Recommendations

6. Salary's effect on career mobility.
7. Family's effect on career mobility.
8. The fact that both partners worked in higher education.
9. Children's effect on relocating.
10. Children's effect on promotion.
11. The number of white male and female administrators on campus.
12. Number of African American males and females supervised.
13. Number of white males and females supervised.
14. Size of budget managed by administrator.
15. Presence of "colored" glass ceiling.
16. Personal obligation to race.
17. Institutional support of recruitment of African American males and females.
18. Adjustments made by coming to present institution.
19. The number of administrators that did not return for current school year.
20. Institution where CEO received undergraduate and doctorate degree.
21. Role of African Americans in institution's hiring process.
22. Shortages of African Americans in higher education affecting the recruitment, retention, promotion of respondent's institution.

As this study of administrators, in the position of dean and above, from HBIs and TWIs additional research is suggested on solely administrators at HBIs. Investigation of additional ethnic populations, cultures, and more is recommended. It is suggested that research on African American women administrators in community colleges be carried out and compared with African American women at four year institutions.

Further research utilizing this methodology is advised for additional exploratory and descriptive research to further supplement the literature on African American women administrators. However, a smaller scale constructed with differently phrased questions is advised.

Obviously, additional research is needed on African American women in higher education. Since this study basically focused on the recruitment, retention, and promotion, there is a need for additional studies to focus on issues of support for these women, (family, friends, institution, and private organizations). The respondents themselves have commented on the issue of additional research and their feelings concerning this survey.

Summary

A discussion of the findings in relation to this study's two essential questions and three guiding questions was presented. Concluding comments on the researcher's initial assumptions and expectations as well as future recommendations from the research were discussed.

Appendices

Appendix A

October 2, 1993

Mr. John Blackburn
American Association of University
Administrators
P.O. Box 31403
Tuscaloosa, AL 35403

Dear Mr. Blackburn,

I am currently conducting research on African American women in higher education as a focus of my dissertation for completion of the doctoral degree in higher education administration. One of my career goals is to increase the amount of research in this area.

As a part of my research efforts, I would like to request from your organization any information, (pre-designed survey instruments or mailing lists) of African American women administrators in the position of dean and above (with and without tenure) at institutions of higher education in the United States.

I would be very appreciative of any information your office may be able to provide on this topic. Please contact me at the following address:

Annette W. Rusher
959 Mallard Creek Road
Louisville, KY 40207

Your response to this request is important to the advancement of research on African American women in higher education.

Sincerely,

Annette W. Rusher

Appendix B

Survey Letter

November 22, 1993

Dear African American Administrator,

Your are aware of the limited amount of research and literature available on African American women in higher education, especially in leadership positions. You are needed to assist in correcting this deficiency. One of my career goals is also to help[increase the research in this area.

As a part of my dissertation research on African American women administrator's recruitment, retention, and promotion patterns I would like to ask you to complete the enclosed survey to be returned by December 10, 1993. My hopes are that is survey will yield valuable information to African American women in all areas of higher education.

This survey should take approximately twenty minutes to complete. Your individual responses will remain confidential. I am interested only in group statistical data.

As an added incentive for completing this survey, you will receive a complementary print, "Symmetry of Hearts" by Brenda Joysmith. This is pictured on front of the survey. In order to receive your print, please return the card enclosed.

Please return the enclosed survey by December 10, 1993:

Annette W. Rusher
959 Mallard Creek Road
Louisville, KY 40207-5808

Your response to this survey is crucial to the advancement of African American women in higher education.

Thank you,

Annette W. Rusher

Enclosures

Appendix C

Complimentary Print Card

COMPLIMENTARY PRINT

Name _____

Address _____

City, State, Zip _____

Please allow 2 - 3 weeks for delivery.

Appendix D

Survey Reminder Card

SURVEY REMINDER

You recently received the Survey of Recruitment, Retention, and Promotion Patterns of African American Women Administrators. If you have already returned it, I appreciate your time. If you have not had the time to complete it, please do so by December 10, 1993.

Appendix E

Subjective Responses of Survey

#87 As you are probably aware some of these questions left room for responses that were not yes or no. If possible I would like to see the results based on responses from other participants in the survey. Good luck as you complete your dissertation. Thank you for the complimentary print symmetry of Heart. It is one of my favorites. Best wishes for a happy holiday season.

#85 This survey was passed on to me by the VP for Student Affairs. I am also ABD in higher education. My dissertation is on the satisfaction level of black graduate/professional students at. I'm comparing differences in satisfaction of those from HBCU and PWI's and male and female. I've had a difficult time getting my surveys returned and it has been very costly. I begin my research (actually my survey research) in Sept and I mailed out 100 surveys. I received about 35 back (after a second mailing). I hope to complete my dissertation by January or early February. I did not receive this survey until Dec. 9th. I hope it helps. I know how frustrating this type of research can be. Good luck my sista. I have only been in this position for three months, however this institution must comply with the Kentucky Plan. While African Americans are recruited. I do not feel that we are promoted (that applies to all PWI's). Therefore, we are not retained for long periods of time. I am interested in the results of your dissertation.

#84 Sexual discrimination, however subtle, does exist, but racial discrimination is more predominately. At an HBC, racial discrimination is not a topic of much discussion, which makes for a much more wholesome work environment—for me. Great idea for a study—please send me a copy of results. Thanks for the print.

#72 I am the associate dean of students. The dean is caucasian and forwarded this to me. There are no African American female or male administrators at the level of dean or above. Please include my data if appropriate, if not we tried. Happy holidays and good luck. Nice presentation. Very flattering. Please let us know when you publish your results. Good luck. We received this Dec. 16th past Dec. 10th date. So we could not get it to you by your date.

#76 Thanks to you and good luck as you pursue your career paths.

#92 Good luck.

#60 Experiences are heavily influenced by the local climate of the institution you work for—Racism, sexism exist. Coping is harder or easier depending on institutional support systems. Ambitious thesis. Good luck.

#63 There is a need for more African American women professional organizations.

#69 I look forward to seeing your results and good luck whatever your endeavors may be.

#56 I wish you success in this project. I would very much like to see a summary of your results.

#59 The administration referred to all report to me. My rapid climb in administration from faculty to president in 8 years is largely due, I think to me being a qualified women and minority. Best wishes.

#49 I work in an HBC environment and many questions in this survey are not applicable.

#48 Given my long history at my institution, I have gradually climbed the ladder to where I presently am one of the senior executives. However, that climb has been more arduous and demanding than those of my white counterparts and their level of productivity is not nearly the same. My situation is somewhat unusual because my longevity has allowed me to forge and create campus alliances that my fellow VPs do not have so I have am unusual power base. Good luck.

#12 It's difficult at best for African American women to advance without a white male mentor. Most of the African American women that I know who are in high level administratie positons have had the benefit of a white male mentor.

#25 I suffered considerable negative behavior. Here, I am the Chief Student Affairs Officer, and yet I don't report directly to the President. The Vice Presidents are all white males and although I am included in their meetings, I have less power, get less respect, am left out of the decison making process on institutional matters, and am not part of their group. I am also not part of the culture that exists outside of them since I'm above everyone else in the hierarchy. I'm in a limbo. I like the students and I like the potential for growth—but I am on the outside looking in. I am very frustrated.

#28 In answer to your request, I must say that if institutions are to recruit and retain African American females, there must be more of a support system. Because most of us are so family oriented, more support for children and family i.e. housing provided must be considered. There is also the fact that so many times there is the one syndrome that we ar totally isolated from the main campus. There needs to be more responsibility and less of the feeling that the university does not have confidence in our abilities. One of the main problems of most AAFA, is the lack of knowledge of how to Network on the campus. This is all too important to get what you want, and know how to do it.

#36 I assumed for questions 34 & 35 you also meant at the level of dean or above. If not limited to dean and above may answers are (34) 315 and (35) 274. I am glad this survey is being done. I had considered conducting similar research myself but never found the time. Thankfully you did. My negative responses regarding career advancement and climate for African American males and females, including myself, are based soley on the current President- the only one I have ever had difficulties with. Fotunately, he alienated many others as well and was finally compelled to resign. I am optimistic things will improve with his departure since other white administrators are much more committed to diversity and affirmative action.

#38 This is great that you're doing this for your thesis, the researach is truly needed as we try to crack the cement ceiling. Mentoring is critical in the recruitment, retention, and promotion of African American women. How can I read your thesis when you finish.

#42 This is an extremely timely and important research project. I would be interested in having a copy of your results. Good luck.

#45 The new wave of college presidents at HBCU's is extremely detrimental to black professionals. I will never, ever work at an HBCU again—not in life. The disrespect and lack of administrating integrity and skills are deplorable. I plan to return to the comprehensive university and never leave. If you think black females lack respect at white universities—try some of the HBCU's. Please maintain the confidentiality which was promised. The promotions referred to occurred under a previous president. Since 1991, I have been demoted to a newly created vice presidency.

#82 Too long!! Good luck with your survey.

#78 The African American female faces two barriers in her efforts to be an effective administrator—racism and sexism. These are daily challenges which often impede the capability of her effectiveness, but these issues are rarely factored into any evaluation of her effectiveness.

#90 I believe that the only way to experience and affect a significant change in the number of African American women in higher education is to encourage each African American woman at the time of entry to college to pursue a career in higher education. This act should initiate a mentoring process which will expose mentees to a network of resources—Each one should reach one of your sisters to effect direct actions and changes. Good luck to your as you pursue your studies. I am interested in reading the results of your research. It should be quite interesting.

#130 Currently at my institution, there are many opportunities for women and African American. Due to the shortage, as well as recent budget cuts, preference is giving to women & minorities in hiring.

#105 Most of my negative responses relate to experiences encountered over the last 1.5 years. For five years the environment was most supportive. The former President and Provost left the Institution. Since they left, I have been making many adjustments. The commitment to diversity and pluralism has begun to diminish. Additionally, as a dean of a primarily white female college, there are many complexities.

#116 The length of this instrument is asking too mcuh of busy advministrator. Your work is important so I've tried.

#118 I appreciate the opportunity to participate in your survey. I think it is noteworthy that as an African American employed by an all women's college which is predominately African American. I had difficulty relating to some of the questions. I do believe taht the experiences in my institution are not representative of other colleges even HBCUs. Additionally, the majority of administrators at my institution are African American females.

#121 I like the cover, please send me a copy. Started to keep it. Best wishes.

#120 My employment is at an HBCU so many of the questions do not apply.

#121 Good survey, I would like to be sent the results of your findings.

#125 It is apparent that we continue to be see as invisible people. Others do not take as seriously and we are basically tolerated. I do not perceive my plight as an African American women administrator any better than the mid 60's.

#135 While positions of leadership in higher education have been male dominated for years, since the late 1970's females have been given somewhat of an opportunity for advancement at this institution. Paradoxically, females have always demonstrated a higher level of competency and leadership than males. In support positions, females were primarily responsible for the implementation of goals and objectives while the males received the credit.

#103 I have enclosed the completed survey about my background, education, and experiences as an African American administrator in higher education. I commend you on selecting a dissertation topic which I feel will yield valuable information and insights. I know you will be busy over the next several months analyzing and reviewing data and completing your dissertation. When you finish, I would be most interested in hearing about the results of your work. I hope you will publish and make presentations at conferences to share what you learn. Best of luck to you as you near the end of your doctoral studies.

Re: promotions—I changed institutions each time. I moved to a higher administrative level. I cannot say that I would not hae been promoted had I stayed, but I was not willing to put in the time to wait and see.

#1 African American women administrators must work extremely hard and demonstrate their relative worth—continuously.

#2 The difficulty in answering #99 is that for me, as a black female—race & sex together have resulted in multiple oppressions.

#4 This is an historically black institution. Some items I answered, did not seem to fit my situation because of the nature of my workplace.

#6 The presentation of this questionnaire made me want to assist you. Good luck on your degree. I remember waiting at the post office for responses to my dissertation questionnaire. When you finish the degree, take three months to read junk novels—nothing heavy! I swear it rebalances your mind. (smile)

#9 Enclosed please find the African American women administrator's recruitment, retention, and promotion patterns survey. I hope the information provided in this survey will be helpful for your dissertation research. Should you need additional information, please do not hesitate to contact me.

#10 Good luck! Would like to see the results.

#11 This was first of all a very attractive survey—The cover itself drew my attention to it and encouraged me to "look inside". Best of luck on your study!

#132 Some questions were difficult to answer because no distinction was made between faculty and professional staff. There are many African American professional staff on campus at a variety of levels, but very few faculty. My case is unique as far as employment here goes. I was recommended for a summer teaching position which led to an administrative position of 15 years duration. Upon completion of the Ph.D. I was recruited for each subsequent position as were the other 2 black female Ph.D.s. However, I do not wish to give the impression that

Appendicies

all is easy and wonderful for everyone here. We have the usual institutional problems. I have just had excellent mentors, both black and white. In the university at large. I am not sure everyone has been as fortunate. Attaining the Ph.D. has made a great difference. Good work is also generally rewarded through compensation.

#131 I hope this information will be useful. Please note that your survey arrived on my campus when you requested it to be returned.

#129 Survey very well done. Good luck! However, several questions were difficult for me to answer because my position as dean is an internal promotion from teaching faculty, I was not recruited and retained in normal sense one may think—I tried to answer all questions.

#17 You omit reference to Hispanics and Asians. On TWI campuses there is more diversity. I supervise 4 Latinos but there was not reference to them. The relationships between and among non-white groups are very important to consider.

#18 The survey was focused on historically white institutions and I found it difficult to respond to some of the questions. I would be interested in seeing the results of your study.

#23 Best of luck on your research. I eagerly wait your results.

#34 #104 contributes but is not the significant factor. It may be helpful to ask to what degree does "shortage contribute. Good luck! I will be interested in your results.

#33 Please share results with me.

#57 I am so sorry that this fell under a pile of papers on my desk. I trust that it reaches you in time to be included. Again, I'm terribly sorry that allowed it to be move down in priority, as I will need to do research of this nature in a couple of years. Good luck!

References

Abney, R., & Richey, D. (1991). Barriers encountered by black female athletic administrators and coaches. *Journal of Physical Education, Recreation and Dance, 62*, 19-21.

Alston, D. (1988). *Recruiting minority classroom teachers: A national challenge.* Washington, DC: National Governor's Association.

Alexander, M.A., & Scott, B.M. (1983). *The AICC perceptive of career management: A strategy for personal and positional power for black women in higher education administration.* Paper presented at the annual conference of the National Association for Women Deans, Administrators, and Counselors, Houston, Texas.

American Council on Education. (1993). *Education ethnicity listing.* Washington, DC: Black Issues in Higher Education.

American Council on Education/Office of Minority Concerns. (1987). *Minorities in higher education (sixth annual status report* . Washington, DC: Carter and Wilson.

Anderson, J. (1988). *Education of blacks in the south: 1860 - 1935* . Chapel Hill: University of North Carolina Press.

Babbie, E. (1990). *The practice of social research (2nd ed.).* California: Wadsworth.

Baker, F.W. (1991). Black faculty in major white higher educational institutions address the need for more minority representation. *Black Issues in Higher Education, 9*(10), 120.

Becker, G. (1957). *The economics of discrimination.* Chicago: University of Chicago.

Becker, G. (1978). *The mad genuis controversy: A study in the sociology of deviance.* Beverly Hills, California: Sage Publications.

Bogden, R. & Biklen, S. (1982). *Qualitative research for education: An introduction to theory and methods.* Boston: Allyn and Bacon.

Biklen, S., & Antler, J. (1990). *Changing education: Women as radicals & conservators.* Albany: State University of New York Press.

Boudon, R. (1988). *The analysis of ideology.* Chicago: University of Chicago Press.

Boudon, Raymond. (1976). Unmarginal devenu un clasique: Paul Lazarsfeld Societe' francaisse de sociologue,*Bulletin* 3, No. 8: 5-7. An obituary article that was first published in *Le Monde*.

Bowles, S. (1972). "Schooling and inequality from generation to generation." *Journal of Political Economy, 80,* 219-251.

Bowles, S., & Gintis, H. (1975). "The problem with human capital theory: A Marxian interpretation." *American Economic Review, Papers and Proceedings, 65,* 74-82.

Bowles, S. (1993). *Markets and democracy: Participation.* Cambridge New York: Cambridge and University Press.

Bowles, S., & Gintis, H. (1986). *Democrates & capitalists: Property, community, and the contradiction of modern social thought.* New York: Basic Books.

Bronfenbrenner, U. (1979). *The ecology of human development.* Cambridge: Harvard University Press.

Brown, S. V. (1987). *Minorities in the graduate education pipeline.* Princeton, NJ: Educational Testing Service.

Carroll, C.M. (1982). *Three's a crowd: The dilemma of the black woman in higher education.* New York: The Feminist Press.

Carter, J.C., & Wilson, R. (1992). *Status report on minorities in higher education* . Washington, DC: American Council on Education.

Chamberlain, M.K. (1991). *Women in academic: Progress and prospects*. New York: Russell Sage.

Cusack, P.A. (1983). *The egalitarian ideal and the American high school.* New York: Longman.

Darity, W. A. (1982). The human capital approach to black-white earnings inequality: Some unsettled questions. *The Journal of Human Resources, 82,* 73-93.

Darity, W. A. (1989). *Race, radicalism, and reform: Selected papers.* New Brunswick USA: Transaction Publishers.

Darling-Hammond, L. (1987). *Career choices for minorities: Who will teach?* Washington, DC: National Education Association and Council of State School Officers.

Davis, A. (1981). Reflections on the Black woman's role in the community of slaves. *Black Scholar,* 12(3), 2-15.

Davis, A. (1989). *Blacks in the federal judiciary: Neutral arbiters or judicial activities.* Bristol, IN: Wyndam Hall Press.

Denzin, N. K., & Lincoln, Y. S. (1994). *Handbook of qualitative research.* Thousand Oaks: Sage Publications.

Denzin, N.K. (1970). The methodologies of symbolic interaction: A critical review of research techniques. In G.P. Stone & H.A. Farberman (Eds.), *Social psychology through symbolic interaction* (pp. 447-456). Walthan, MA: Xerox College publishing.

Doeringer, P.B., & Piore, M. J. (1972). *Internal labor markets and manpower analysis.* Lexington, MA: D.C. Heath.

Doeringer, P. B. (1990). *Bridges to retirement: Older workers in a changing labor market.* Ithaca, New York: School of Industrial Relations and Labor.

Doyle, W. (1979). Classroom tasks and students abilities. In P. L. Peterson & H. J. Walberg (Eds.), Research on teaching: Concepts, findings and implications (pp, 183-209). Berkley: McCutchan.

Dumas, R. (1980). *Dilemmas of black females in leadership.* In L. Rodgers-Rose (Ed.), The black woman (pp. 201-215). California: Sage Publications.

Epstein, C. F. (1973, August). Black and female, the double whammy. *Psychology Today, 89,* 57-61.

References

Epstein, C. F. (1987). *Multiple demands and multiple roles: The conditions of successful management.* In F. J. Crosby (Ed.), Spouse, worker, parent: On gender and multiple roles (pp. 23-25). New Haven: Yale University Press.

Epstein, C. F. (1993). *Women in law.* Urbana: University of Illinois Press.

Erickson, F. (1982). Classroom discourse as improvisation: Relationships between academic task structure and social participating structure in lessons. In L.C. Wilkinson (Ed.), *Communicating in the classroom.* New York: Academic Press.

Erickson, F. (1986). Qualitative methods in research on teaching. In M.C. Wittrock (Ed.), *Handbook of research on teaching (3rd ed.)* (pp. 119-161).

Erickson, F., & Linn, R. L. (1990). *Quantitative Methodology.* American Educational Research Association. New York: MacMillian Publishers. 125

Ford Foundation. (1977). *Women and minorities of higher education institutions: Employment patterns and salary comparisons.* A Special Study Supported by Ford Foundation. Washington, DC: Alstyne, Withers, and Mensel.

Ford Foundation. (1989). *Black women in academe: Issues and strategies: In association of American colleges*. Project on the status and Education of Women. New York: Moses.

Foster, R. & Wilson, P. (1942). *Women after college.* New York: Columbia University Press.

Foster, R. (1944). *Marriage and family relationships.* New York: MacMillian Publishers.

Fosu, A. K. (1992). Occupational mobility of black women, 1958- 1981: The impact of post-1964 antidiscrimination measures. *Industrial and Labor Relations Review, 45,* 281-294.

Freeman, R. B. (1973). *"Changes in the labor market for black Americans, 1948-1972."* Brookings Papers on Economic Activity, 67-132.

Garibaldi, A. (1988). The paradoxical impact of affirmation action on the supply of black teachers. *Educational Policy, 2,* 177-188.

Giddings, P. (1985). *When and where I enter.* New York: Bantam Books.

Gill, G., & Showell, B. (1991). *The cinderella concept of the black female in higher education*. Washington, DC: Howard Press.

Gobal, M. H. (1964). *An introduction of research procedure in social sciences.* New York: Asia Publishing.

Graham, P. (1987, April). Black teachers: A drastically scare resource. *Phi Delta Kappa, 68,* 598-605.

Green, J. L. & Wallet, C. (Eds.). (1981). *Ethnography and language in educational settings.* Norwood, NJ: Ablex Publishing Corporation.

Guba, E. G. (1990). The paradigm dialog. Newburg Park, CA: Sage Publications.

Guba, E. G., & Lincoln, Y.S. (1982). *Causality vs. plausibility: Alternative stances for inquiry into human behavior.* Paper presented at the annual meeting of the American Educational Research Association.

Harten, C.C., Moden, G.O., & Wilson, P.A. (1989). Women and minority professional staff in student personnel: A census and analysis. *NASPA Journal, 26*, 43-50.

Harvard, P.A. (1986). Successful behaviors by black women administrators in higher education: Implications for leadership. Paper presented at leadership conference for minority women. San Francisco, CA.

Heckman, J. J., & Payner, B. S. (1989). "Determining the impact of federal antidiscrimination policy on the economic status on blacks: A study of South Carolina." *American Economic Review, 79*, 138-177.

Hill, R. B. (1978). *The illusion of black progress.* Washington; National Urban League Research Department.

Hill, R. B., & Billingsby, A. (1993). *Research on the African American family: A holistic perspective.* Westport, CN: Auburn House.

Hinkle, D., Wiersma, W., and Jurs, S. (1979). *Applied statistics for the behavioral sciences.* Boston: Houghton Mifflin.

Hoskin, R. L. (1978). *Black administrators in higher education: Conditions and perceptions.* New York: Praeger Publishers.

Hyman, H. H. (1955). *Survey design and analysis: Principles, cases, and procedures with a forward by Paul F. Lazarsfeld.* Glencoe, IL: Free Press.

Hyman, H. H., O'Gorman, H.J. & Bay C. (1988). *Surveying social life: Paper in honor of H. H. Hyman.* Middletown, CT: Wesleyan University Press.

Irvin, J. (1988) A analysis of the problem of disappearing black educators. *Elementary School Journal, 88*, 503-513.

Johnson, M. (1991, October). *A survey of factors affecting workplace performance and career advancement of black women administrators.* Paper presented at league for Innovation in the Community College "leadership 2000" Conference, Chicago, IL.

Jones, R.F., & Thompson, S. (1991). *Role-perception of minority admission professionals: History of minority admissions administrators on predominantly white campus.* Chicago, IL: University of Chicago. (ERIC Document Reproduction Service No. ED 338 174).

Kanter, R. M. (1977). *Men and women of the corporation.* New York: Books, Inc.

Kanter, R. M., Stein, B., & Jick, T. (1992). *The challenge of organizational change: How companies experience it and leaders guide it.* New York: Maxwell MacMillian International Publishers.

Konrad, A.M., & Pfeffer, J. (1991). Understanding the hiring of women and minorities in educational institutions. *Sociology of Education, 64(3)*, 141-157.

Krueger, A. O. (1963). "The economics of discrimination." *Journal of Political Economy, 71*, 481-486.

Krueger, A. O., & Ito, T. (1993). *Trade and protectionism.* Chicago: University of Chicago Press.

Kunjufu, J. (1982-1990). *Countering the conspiracy to destroy black boys (Vols. 1-3).* Chicago: African American Images.

Kunjufu, J. (1991). *Black economics: Solutions for economic and minority empowerment.* Chicago, IL: African American Images.

Kyle, D. W. (1979). *Life-as-teacher: The disclosure of teachers' activities and emergent problems.* Unpublished doctoral dissertation, University of Virginia, Virginia.

Leibowitz, A. (1974). "Home investments in children." *Journal of Political Economy, 82,* 111-131.

Leibowitz, A. (1982). Federal recognition of the rights of minority language groups. *National Clearinghouse Bilingual Education, 218,* 23.

Leigh, D. E., & Rawlins, V. L. (1974). "Racial differentials in male unemployment rates: Evidence from low-income urban areas." *Review of Economics and Statistics, 56,* 150-157.

Lightfoot, S. L. (1983). *The good high school: Portraits of character culture.* New York: Basic Books.

Lightfoot, S. L. (1988). *Balm in gilead: Journey of a healer.* Massuchusetts: Aadrean Publishing Company.

Lofland , J. & Lofland, L. H. (1984). *Analyzing social settings (2nd ed.).* Belmont, CA: Wadsworth Publishing Company.

Lofland, J. & Lofland, L. H. (1993). *Polite protesters: The America peace movement of the 1980s.* Syracuse, New York: Syracuse University Press.

Marshall, R. (1974). "The economics of racial discrimination: A survey." *Journal of Economic Literature, 12,* 849-871.

Marshall, R. (1987). *Unheard voices: Labor and economic policy in a competitive world.* New York: Basic Books.

Mazon, M. R., & Ross, H. (1990). Equality of educational opportunity: Myths and realities. *The Western Journal of Black Studies, 14,* 159-164.

Mercer, J. (1992). Presidential revolving door disproportionately hurts HBCs and weakens stability, leaders say. *Black Issues in Higher Education, 9(1),* 20-22.

Moore, K. (1981). Leaders in Transition Survey developed by the Center for the Study of Higher Education at Penn State.

Moses, M. H. (1980, March). Black women administrators in higher education: An endangered species. *Journal of Black Studies, 10,* 195-210.

Noble, J.L. (1956). *The Negro woman's college education.* New York: Bureau of Publications.

Office of Women in Higher Education (1988). *Women chief executive affairs in U.S. colleges and universities.* Washington, DC: American Council on Education.

Ogbu, J. (1978). *Minority education and caste: The American system in cross-cultural perspective.* New York: Academic Press.

Ogbu, J., & Gibson, M. A. (1991). *Status and schooling: A comparative study of immigrant and involuntary minority.* New York: Garland.

Palonsky, S.B. (1986). Ethnographic scholarship and social education. Paper presented at the annual meeting of the College and University Faculty Assembly, National Council for Social Studies, New York.

Patton, M. Q. (1980). *Qualitative evaluation methods.* Beverly Hills: Sage Publications.

Patton, M. Q. (1990). *Qualitative evaluation and research methods.* Newbury Park, CA: Sage Publishers.

Phillip, M.C. (1993). Women leadership and the academy: There's still a long way to go. *Black Issues in Higher Education, 10,* 32-33.

Powell, G. N. (1987). *Women and men in management.* California: Sage Publications.

Rea, L. M. (1992). *Designing and conducting survey research: A comprehensive guide.* San Francisco: Jossey-Bass.

Reynolds, M. (1973). *"Economic theory and racial wage differentials."* Institute for Research on Poverty Discussion Paper 1974-1973, University of Wisconsin.

Reynolds, M. (1987). *Making america poorer: The cost of labor law.* Washington, DC: Cato Institutions.

Rist, R. C. (1983). On the application of qualitative research to the policy process: An emergent linkage.

Rist, R. C. (1990). *Program evaluation and the management of government.* New Brunswick: Transaction Publishers.

Ross, M. (1993). *1993 survey report on the American college president.* Washington, DC: American Council on Education.

Rubery, J. (1978). "Structured labor markets, worker organization and low pay." Cambridge Journal of Economics.

Rubery, J., Castro, A., & Mehaut, P. (1992). *International integration and labour market organizations.* London: San Diego: Academic Press.

Smith, J. P., & Welch, F. (1975). *Black-white male earnings and employment 1960-1970."* R-1666, Santa Monica, CA: Rand Corporation.

Smith, J.P., & Welch, F. (1986). *Closing the gap: forty years of economic progress for blacks.* Santa Monica, CA: Rand Corporation, US Department of Labor.

Sowell, T. (1971). "Economics and black people." *Review of Black Political Economy (1),* 3-21.

Sowell, T. (1993). *Inside America education: The decline, the deception, the dogmas.* New York: Free Press; Toronto: Maxwell MacMillian.

Tack, M. W., & Patitu, C. L. (1992). *Faculty job satisfaction: Women and minorities in Peril.* ERIC Clearinghouse on Higher Education: Washington, DC: The George Washington University.

Tobin, M. (1981). *The black female PH.D.: Education and career development.* Boston: University Press.

Traudt, P. J. (1981, May). *Instructional approaches to qualitative research methods.* Paper presented at the annual meeting of the International Communication Association, Minneapolis.

Waller, W. (1932). *The sociology of teaching.* New York: John Wiley.

Waller, W., & Goode, W. J. (1970). *On the family, education, and war.* Chicago: University of Chicago Press.

Williams, B.M. (1986). Black woman: Assertiveness vs. Aggressiveness. *Journal of Afro American Issues, 3,* 204-211.

Willie, C., Hope, R. O., & Grady, M. K. (1991). *African American and the doctoral experience: Implications for policy.* New York: Teacher's College Press.

Wilson, R. (1987). *Recruitment and retention of minority faculty and staff.* Washington, DC: American Council on Education.

Witt, E. (1982, 1988). *The supreme court and individual rights.* Washington, DC: Congressional Quarterly.

Wolcott, H.F. (1977). *Teachers versus technocrats: An educational innovation in anthropological perspective.* Eugene, OR: University of Oregon, Center for Educational Policy Management.

Wolcott, H. F. (1990). *Writing up qualitative research.* Newbury Park, CA: Sage Publishers.

About the Author

Author, Annette Williams Rusher, is the seventh child of seven children (Herman, Wendolyn, Beverly, Joseph, Myra, and Delphine) of Alonzo Williams and Annie Mae Williams (both deceased). She was born August 9, 1956 in Oklahoma City, Oklahoma.

She received her early and secondary education in Oklahoma City Public Schools. In 1974, she entered Oscar Rose Junior College in Midwest City, Oklahoma. In 1976, she transferred to the University of Oklahoma in Norman, Oklahoma and earned a Bachelor or Arts degree in Psychology in 1980. In 1981, she married Lt. Robert Ellis Rusher, moved to Fort Knox, Kentucky for a short period, and then on to Kirchgoens, Germany , Saudi Arabia, Turkey and France where she lived from 1982 to 1985. She has travelled extensively throughout Europe, the Middle East, the Caribbean, Korea , Canada, and the United States.

Between 1985 and 1991, she and her husband returned to the United States to lived at Fort Knox, Kentucky, she became education coordinator for the Army Family Advocacy Program, began work on her Master of Arts in Education (community and agency counseling) from Western Kentucky University, and received her degree in 1991. In 1991 she resigned her position as education coordinator and began to work on her doctoral degree full time at the University of Louisville. Dr. Rusher completed her Ed.D. degree in August 1994 in Educational Counseling Psychology and Student Personnel Services.

The research on African American women in higher education was her doctoral dissertation work. She recently accepted a research position with Richland College, Dallas, Texas in the Office of Institutional Research.